Personal power doesn't come from trying to
control external events and other people.
A person cannot do what cannot be done.
Life is not a matter to be managed.
We have little influence on its outcome.
Our only impact lies in how we live it.
We didn't ask for the responsibility of taking
charge of ourselves, but it's the only power
to which we are entitled. And, in the end, no
matter how well we have prepared, the
moment belongs to God.

—From chapter 12

Other Books by Sheldon Kopp

GURU
IF YOU MEET THE BUDDHA ON THE ROAD, KILL HIM!
THE HANGED MAN
NO HIDDEN MEANINGS (with Claire Flanders)
THIS SIDE OF TRAGEDY
THE NAKED THERAPIST
BACK TO ONE
AN END TO INNOCENCE
WHAT TOOK YOU SO LONG (with Claire Flanders)
MIRROR, MASK, AND SHADOW
THE PICKPOCKET AND THE SAINT
EVEN A STONE CAN BE A TEACHER
HERE I AM, WASN'T I!
WHO AM I . . . , REALLY?
RAISE YOUR RIGHT HAND AGAINST FEAR,
EXTEND THE OTHER IN COMPASSION

ROCK PAPER SCISSORS

Understanding the Paradoxes of Personal Power
and Taking Charge of Our Lives

Sheldon Kopp

CompCare Publishers

2415 Annapolis Lane
Minneapolis, Minnesota 55441

Kopp, Sheldon B., 1929-
    Rock, paper, scissors / by Sheldon Kopp.
        p. cm.
    Includes bibliographical references.
    ISBN 0-89638-193-5: $8.95
    1. Control (Psychology) 2. Helplessness (Psychology)
3. Interpersonal relations. I. Title
BF611.K64   1989
158--dc20   89-22139
                                                    CIP

Cover and interior design by Susan Rinek.

    Inquiries, orders, and catalog requests should be addressed to
    CompCare Publishers
    2415 Annapolis Lane
    Minneapolis, MN 55441
    Call toll free 800/328-3330
    (Minnesota residents 612/559-4800)

5   4   3   2   1
93   92   91   90   89

All accounts of patients are disguised to protect their privacy. In some instances, the portraits I have presented are composites and in others, identifying biographical details have been either omitted or changed.

Contents

Prologue

A tale is told of an old man who lived a quiet life in a simple cottage, until one day his village was over-run by Nazi occupation forces.[1] A storm trooper dragged the old man out into the street and told him, "From now on, you will let me live in your house, and every day you will serve my meals, make my bed, and shine my boots. Otherwise, I will kill you. Will you do as you're told?" The old man did not answer.

The storm trooper took over the cottage and the helpless old man served him his meals every day, made his bed, and shined his boots. For two years he obeyed every order with one exception—he would not say a word.

Then one day, the allied armies liberated the village. As they dragged the storm trooper from the cottage, the old man took a deep breath and finally answered the question: "No!"

1

Both a Crown and a Cross

No matter how powerful we are, or imagine ourselves to be, some people are stronger. However powerless we may feel, others are weaker. This continuous spiralling of advantage and obstacle, strength and weakness reminds me of a game I often played as a child—a game called "Rock, Paper, Scissors."

It is a hand game, best played between two people. At the count of three, each player puts out a hand in one of three positions: palm up and out flat, representing a piece of paper, in a closed fist that represents a rock, or with the second and third fingers extended, indicating a pair of scissors.

The wonder of the game is that each choice—rock, paper, or scissors—can mean either victory or defeat, depending on what it's up against. Paper covers rock, rock breaks scissors, scissors cut paper, and so it goes, round and round. Winning alternates with losing according to the situation just as power alternates with powerlessness in unresolvable paradox.

Like so many other human assets, power can be a crown or a cross. When we have power we receive an abundance of valued goods and privileges, an elevated position admired by others, and increased freedom to do as we please. Our sense of well-being is expanded, so that we may be generous toward others who have little; we may even work for causes aimed at increasing the well-being of those less fortunate.

Paradoxically, possessing power may inflate our sense of self-importance, and so encourage us to exploit other people. The temptation to take ourselves too seriously when we feel powerful is illustrated in a sixteenth-century Chinese folk novel that retells an ancient legend of a popular culture-hero called Monkey.[1]

Born out of a symbolically strong stone egg, Monkey was immediately elected king of the monkeys. In an attempt to attain understanding of everything he might see or hear, and mastery of any obstacle he might encounter, Monkey studied with a Taoist magician who taught him many magical skills, including how to change himself into seventy-two different shapes and how to turn a somersault that could carry him six thousand miles. Eventually Monkey became so impressed with his own miraculous powers that his inflated sense of self-importance reduced his heroic undertakings to reckless misadventures of the sort that sometimes make monkeys of us all.

This satirical tale is an imaginative re-creation of an actual seventh-century religious pilgrimage undertaken by a Buddhist monk named Tripitaka, who travelled overland to India to recover a vast collection of holy writings. In the retelling of the story of this journey, the monk is accompanied by the magically gifted monkey-protector whose fantastic exploits exaggeratedly parallel the legendary historical adventure.

Tripitaka represents the unpretentious human spirit free of the heroics that often accompany extraordinary powers. He was easy prey both to external forces, and to those of his inner misgivings. Monkey was his shamelessly prideful and intensely ambitious shadow aspect. Together they faced one challenge after another.

Monkey never faltered in his overconfident expectation that he could easily overcome all obstacles. There was no adversary too powerful for him to take on. He even set off to challenge the Jade Emperor's reign over the blessed realms of Heaven. Monkey reached the border of that sacred territory only to find himself standing before the Buddha. When the Enlightened One challenged this upstart's claim to power, Monkey arrogantly asserted that he could easily demonstrate how fit he was to be seated on the throne of Heaven.

To instruct him in humility, the Enlightened One wagered that Monkey didn't even have the power to jump off the palm of Buddha's right hand. The terms of the wager were that if Monkey suceeded, he would win his seat on Heaven's throne, but if he failed, he would have to return to earth to do a long, long penance.

Monkey thought to himself, "This Buddha is a perfect fool. His palm is no more than eight inches across. I have the power to somersault over six thousand miles. How could I possibly fail to jump clear of it?"

Buddha stretched out his right hand and Monkey leaped off with all of his might. He flew so far and so fast that he felt certain he would win the wager. When he landed at the foot of five pink mountains sticking straight up into the air, Monkey was sure that he had reached the end of the world. Before returning to the Buddha to claim his forfeit, he decided it might be wise to leave evidence of how far he had come.

To mark the territory, Monkey went to the top of each of the mountains and urinated on its peak. When he went back to the Buddha, he boasted about having gone to the ends of the earth and suggested that the Enlightened One examine the evidence he had left on each of the sky-high mountain peaks.

Smiling sweetly, the Buddha opened his right hand. At the tip of each of his five fingers was a tiny yellow puddle.

Monkey's arrogance depended on his controlling others by besting them in contests, and impressing them by displaying his powers. In contrast, Tripitaka made his way one step at a time, modestly knowing that he would win some contests and lose others. During all his inevitable ups and downs, the modest monk held onto the sense of inner power that came with taking charge of his life while patiently and responsibly pursuing a pilgrimage that he understood was well suited to the decent, fallible person he knew himself to be.

Triumphs that afford a sense of well-being, strength, and confidence that can serve us well and be a boon to those around us may also make us arrogant and encourage us to act outrageously. The attainment of power can corrupt our character with inconsiderate, exploitive, and abusive attitudes that tempt us to brag, show off, and otherwise attempt to make ourselves feel that we matter more by making others appear to matter less.

For some people, self-esteem depends on seeing themselves as powerful. When life inevitably exposes their inadequacies and ordinariness, they experience distress that seems unbearable. *To learn to use power well—or to profit from it when it is ours—we must give up trying to control others, and instead enjoy the freedom power affords by responsibly taking charge of ourselves.*

Those who are gifted with intelligence, talent, physical beauty, and charismatic appeal have easier access than ordinary people to the power perks of wealth, fame, and influence. Paradoxically, some of these well-endowed achievers attain public greatness but are unable to run their private lives successfully. The failed marriages, alcoholism, suicide, or madness of world-class celebrities like Howard Hughes, Marilyn Monroe and Sylvia Plath illustrate that the wealth, acclaim, and artistry of professional success do not preclude failure on a personal level.

For some achievers, it is simply impossible to live up to an overly idealized public image. The recent discrediting of television evangelists such as Jim Bakker and Jimmy Swaggart shows how charismatic fame can be reduced to scandalous notoriety when human weaknesses are brought to light.

Some social reformers, political leaders, and riders of the holy-man circuit treat their home lives as no more than scheduling problems. And some social, political, and spiritual leaders who seemed able to change history single-handedly turned out to be incapable of managing more domestic matters of heart and hearth.

Examples range from the sublime to the ridiculous. Mahatma Gandhi freed a subcontinent but could not maintain a satisfying family life. Abraham Lincoln settled a conflict that divided a nation, but lived a deeply depressed personal life. Werner Ehrhardt established the est Seminars, a process aimed at freeing others to act responsibly, but not before deserting his wife and children. Fritz Perls suffered the same sort of failures while founding the revolutionary Gestalt therapy approach to unifying personality.

The Bible abounds in archetypal examples of spiritual leaders and other divinely chosen figures who had everything—everything, that is, except personal fulfillment. Abraham, Samson, Solomon, Moses, and even Jesus exercised spiritual power but at the cost of sacrificing more mundane personal fulfillment.

Some of these paradoxes seem inherent in the possession of power. Others are acquired. In my own upbringing, questions of power were filled with contradictions. My mother often admonished me, "Nobody loves a loser!", but whenever I succeeded at something, my achievements simply confirmed her assumption that nothing I could accomplish was worth doing.

When I was sixteen, I bought a second hand guitar for eighteen dollars. I paid for both the instrument and for music lessons out of my own after-school earnings.

After six months of study and practice, I understood something about music theory, and more important, I had increased my enjoyment of listening to music. Satisfied that I had attained all I had set out to do, I gave up taking lessons and resold the guitar for exactly the amount it had cost me. I felt very proud of all that I had accomplished. My mother knew that I had never intended to become a professional performer. And yet her response was, "Everything you try ends up in failure!"

My father summed up his attitudes about any display of success by saying, "Never blow your own horn or other people will resent your achievements." He had declined a position of partnership in the firm for which he worked because "everyone hates the boss."

My intellectual achievements were also subjected to criticism born of his false modesty. My father had grown up in a family so poor that he was forced to drop out of school in sixth grade. Having gone on to educate himself by reading whatever books he could beg, borrow, or steal, he read to me often and inscribed every volume he bought me with the adage, "Books are your best friends!"

He taught me a great deal about nontraditional ideas gleaned from the writings of Marx, Darwin, H.G. Wells, and Plato. During my discipleship, he seemed very pleased with how well I learned and was proud that I wanted to go on to college. But as my education took on a direction of its own, our dialectical talks soured.

During the time when our discussions often ended up with his answering my questions by citing some of his favorite texts, he enjoyed our intellectual exchanges. As I grew, inevitably there came a time when I challenged his beliefs, documenting my arguments with references to texts that I had read and he had not. All at once his operative adage, "Books are your best friends" was replaced by the contradictory, "Experience is the best teacher."

My mother had never made much of the power of my intelligence. She measured achievement in monetary terms. Her challenge to my claim of intellectual power was, "If you're so smart, how come you're not rich?"

Like my father, she also encouraged me to get an education, but mainly so that I could acquire wealth. She bought me many little luxuries, always with the admonition, "Today I'll give you a taste of sweet things; tomorrow you'll make sure to earn enough money to get them for yourself." And if I didn't get the education that would guarantee me a well-paying professional position, she suggested I keep in mind that "it's as easy to fall in love with a rich girl as a poor one."

In any case, there was never any question of my gaining ascendancy over her authority because "parents, teachers, and other grown-ups always know what's best for children." Even once I grew up, she assured me that my power would never equal hers because, "No matter what kind of big shot you might think you've become, you'll always be my little boy." To which she added enigmatically, "When you become a mother, then you'll understand!"

The trek through the paradoxes of power is tough enough without our having any useless baggage to bear. It helps to begin by substituting flexible adult guidelines for the rigid rules acquired in childhood. If we want personal freedom, we must learn to temper appreciation for power when we have it with respect for others when they don't.

2

Control Is a Cord
Tied at Both Ends

Some of my most memorable experiences of both
power and helplessness occurred while raising my
three sons. As toddlers, each child subjected me to a
crash course in power plays by testing the limits of
my parental authority. During those preschool years,
if I told one of them to do something, he frequently
said, "No!" and, if I insisted that he share, he usually
answered, "Mine!"

Whenever I demonstrated that I was bigger, he
set out to prove that his will was stronger. He had an
unfair advantage. Not only was he more innately
appealing to me than I was to him, we were both
completely committed to his happiness.

As infants, each of our children had developed
an inflated sense of influence on his environment.
Simply by crying out, he could count on being fed
when he was hungry, warmed when he was cold,
and comforted when he felt distress. But once he
learned to stand on his own two feet and began to
explore the world around him, he encountered unex-

pected challenges to his infantile fantasy of omnipotence. There were doors he could not open, objects he could not reach, and perhaps worst of all, parents who sometimes stopped him from doing as he pleased. Rather than surrender his power, he stubbornly insisted on having his own way.

During those "terrible two's," I tried to preempt each toddler's testing of the limits of my power by offering him a choice between alternatives that were acceptable to me. For example, at mealtime, I would attempt to maintain control by asking him cleverly whether he wanted to put away his toys *before or after* eating.

Often he eluded *my* attempt at defining our relationship by *his* simple and stubborn assertion, "No eat, just play!" Often the majesty of my assumed authority was effectively deflated. More times than I care to recall, I surrendered to setting his toys aside myself, picked him up, and seated him at the dining-room table.

Once seated, he displayed passive resistance that easily shattered any illusion that I had restored my dominance. My parental responsibility for seeing to it that he was properly cared for required that I submit to waiting him out while he played with his food and then cleaning up the mess he had made of the meal.

I was delighted when each of my sons outgrew the toddler rebellion and went on to develop some semblance of socialization. My misplaced complacency made me believe I would be better prepared to cope with his emergence into the boy/man struggles of adolescence. At that point, each of my teenage sons offered me a refresher course in power plays by devoting himself wholeheartedly to the assertion of his individual autonomy.

Having weathered the early years of fatherhood, I was on the alert. When each son reached thirteen, I sat him down for a ritual father-and-son talk. Mostly I talked and he listened while I assured him that over the next four or five years, it would be his task to display increasing resistance to my authority over him and predicted that during these power struggles sometimes we would get so angry, it might be hard to remember how much we loved one another.

I pledged that while waiting for him to become grown up enough to decide everything for himself, I would do all I could to keep him under my protective control. Until then, I urged him to argue with me whenever he felt that he knew best. I promised to gradually give up being the boss and predicted that eventually he would overthrow my authority to take full charge of his own life.

Until then, each of my sons would have to endure my telling him what he could and could not do. In the process, he would learn from my behavior that power over others is the ability to determine what happens by getting others to do what we want. He would come to understand that we can control other people's behavior by threatening or punishing, by promising or rewarding, or by talking them into our way of thinking.

I explained that when there is not enough good stuff to go around, we sometimes see competitive power plays as the only way to get our share. I went on to point out that when some of us are not yet strong or grown up enough to take care of ourselves, we have to agree that the ones who are in charge have to take responsibility for what happens to the younger, weaker ones.

I hoped that by paying attention to what went on in the world outside our home, he would also come to learn that of all God's creatures, only we humans regularly exploit and destroy our own kind. People take much longer than animals to grow up and become independent of their parents. Another way that people differ from animals is that they enjoy thinking of themselves as powerful. As a result, many human adults try to make up for having depended on others for so long by pushing around people who are not as powerful.

I was less interested in encouraging my sons to attain *power over others* than in their developing the self-confidence that comes with developing the *inner power* that would offer protection from other people's determining what happened to them. That sort of self-direction is experienced as feeling in charge of our lives in ways that allow us the freedom to do as we please.

When people have power over others, often they feel self-important and pleased that they can get things others don't have. .Unfortunately, these advantages usually make them feel that people who are not as powerful don't matter as much as they do. When we have power over others, it's easy to ignore the needs of those who remain helpless.

Whether too much or too little, power over others is always a problem. It is often said that "power corrupts".[1] That old adage may be accurate but *"the absence of power also corrupts!"*[2] Whether the external power structure is maintained by stick, carrot, or mind-bending rhetoric, the oppressors usually blame the victims, and, too often, the victims blame themselves.

The effect of having power on the people who have it is not always good; the effect of not having power on those who are powerless is not always bad. In the long run, the way we *react to* having or not having power can be more consequential than what we get to do with our power or don't get to do without it. These paradoxical effects are not always obvious or recognized, so unwittingly—whether power and powerlessness are real or imagined—we may react in ways that make us needlessly unhappy. When we understand this, we are freer to avoid traps of dominance and submission and instead to seek real, personal, inner power so that we can enjoy the happiness that comes from being in charge of ourselves.

The evil effects of power that can come from either end of the spectrum were demonstrated in the chilling outcome of an often referred to social psychological study conducted some years ago at Stanford University.[3] A simulated prison was set up in the basement of the psychology department building. The normal young male college students hired as experimental subjects were arbitrarily assigned the role of guard or prisoner. The study started out as a two-week-long investigation of the psychological impact of incarceration on the subjects who served as the prisoners.

Before the end of the first week, unexpectedly

terrifying results necessitated abortive termination of the study. Even a simulated power structure, with polarities as extreme as that of a prison situation, proved so destructive that the investigators decided to present their findings to the U.S. House of Representatives' Committee on the Judiciary.

By the sixth day of the study, the subjects could no longer distinguish their personal values from those engendered by their pretended positions of power. Many of the guards had become sadistically tyrannical in their arbitrary abuse of the mock authority that they had been assigned. There were some guards whose character appeared better able to withstand the damaging effects of the play-acting. But even those who did not actively tyrannize the designated inmates would not interfere with the abusive behavior of the other guards.

The undermining of standards of personal decency was not restricted to the simulated power structure's impact on the attitudes and actions of those students who had been assigned the status of authority. The spirit and the ethics of the disempowered prisoners were as quickly and irrevocably corrupted as those of the guards.

Arbitrary assignment of reciprocal roles in an artificial power structure selectively determined how the corruption would be manifested in each group's respective belief system. The behavior of the guards was rigid and cruel. When pressured, they colluded as accomplices who covered for one another. The prisoners' reactions ranged from panic to depression. Under stress, they often betrayed one another.

If we are to avoid the pitfalls of power that tempt us

to betray ourselves and one another, we must learn to rec-
ognize the temptations to corruption inherent in both
dominance and submission.

In the chapters that follow, we will explore ways
of remaining in charge of ourselves that do *not*
require controlling other people. Ironically whether
our power is great or small, real or imagined, its
effects can make decency difficult to maintain. Even
so, living well is not out of the question. First we
must learn to recognize the polarities posed by both
posession and lack of power. Only then can we discover better ways to cope with its presence or
absence.

The way we feel and how we behave may pivot
on the power we *attribute* to one another. Often we
act as if there was just so much power to go around.
If one of us has it, the other must be proportionally
powerless. We must learn to distinguish those times
when we feel either stronger or weaker than we actually are from situations when we or others actually
have the upper hand because of being able to inflict
painful punishments or offer valued rewards.

If actual oppression and exploitation are to be
alleviated, those who hold *real* power have to recognize the value of more democratic rule. And objec-
tively powerless people must join together in
cooperative coalitions that compel redistribution of
limited resources and offer opportunities for influencing otherwise inaccessible authorities. On the
other hand, unwarranted *imagined* power and powerlessness can only be ameliorated if we are able to
make changes in our individual attitudes.

There are situations in which we must learn to

cope with the responsibility of having authority over other people, and there are situations when our power is limited by helpless dependence on those in charge. For all of us, subjective experiences of power and helplessness began in infancy. The power crises inherent throughout childhood recur in adults at times of overwhelming stress and debilitation. As children, we learned to manage both our earliest infantile illusions of omnipotence and our later sense of powerlessness. Unfortunately, some of these techniques may endure into adulthood. These anachronistic outlooks can cause adults to experience power struggles where none exist, and to imagine themselves in situations so overwhelming that they either overlook or exaggerate both their actual emotional freedom, and their effective impact on others.

The paradoxes of power relationships are insidious. We'd like to believe that having power offers uncomplicated advantages, but a popular limerick points up the give-and-take of both high and low places in the hierarchy:

> *Big fleas have little fleas*
> *upon their backs to bite 'em,*
> *And little fleas have lesser fleas,*
> *and so* ad infinitum.

The pyramid of power is an endless interweaving of freedom and constraint. I remember with embarassment my own early lack of awaress of the pitfalls inherent in the power hierarchy I so innocently entered at the beginning of my professional career.

After ten days on the job, the explosive impact of

the locked psychiatric ward's security door slamming shut behind me still came as a shock. As I approached the control center, the dull rattle of the tarnished, oversized keys that dangled from my belt had a curiously calming effect. Attempting to appear more in charge of myself than I actually felt, I ordered a veteran floor-nurse to hurry up and fetch the psychiatric patient I had come to interview.

One of the nurse's regular duties was to assist in the grooming of inexperienced mental-health trainees like me. She must have understood that confirmation of whatever authority I assumed depended on her cooperation. The nurse rushed off to find the patient I had summoned. *She did as she was told.*

I was an unseasoned intern, not yet twenty-three years old. The patient was a middle-aged man accused of indecent exposure. Before his involuntary hospitalization for a month of psychiatric observation, he had been the head of a family and a successful store manager.

My supervisor had instructed me in advance about the information I was to obtain in this intake interview. I introduced myself by title, addressed the patient by his first name, and began to question him. *I did as I was told.*

Within the first few minutes of our meeting, I asked this man I'd never met before to describe his sex life with his wife, and to tell me how often he masturbated. Despite his obvious embarrassment, the patient obediently answered every question I asked. *He also did as he was told.*

We must learn to take responsibility for both our power and our helplessness. It sounds simple, but it isn't easy!

We all need to carry seemingly contradictory reminders in two pockets and, according to the needs of the moment, we must reach into one or the other. In the right pocket are the words, *"For my sake, God created the universe"* and in the left, *"I am dust and ashes."*

3

Even the Appearance of Power

Power is the ability to determine what happens. But simply seeming powerful can add to the impact of an organization or an individual. As Hobbes pointed out, "The reputation for power *is* power." If we are seen as important people, we can influence others merely by extending or withholding access and approval.

The ambiguities of the experience of personal power played havoc for me midway through the development of my career. I was sufficiently seasoned to have secured some confidence in my own competence as a psychotherapist, but I was not yet far enough along to have attained the professional recognition that eventually provided me with a reputation for power.

I attended a week-long workshop of the American Academy of Psychotherapists, a wide-ranging gathering of well-known older gurus and unknown younger disciples who alternately met in encounter groups and watched each other work with patients. I was very anxious about how I might appear in the eyes of the celebrated clinicians whose writings had long influenced my work.

There were many other young therapists attending the workshop whose midcareer positions were as unclearly established as my own. Because of anxiety about my status, I focused my attention selectively on the top and bottom of the power pyramid. Ignoring my peers, I listened admiringly to the charismatic founders of their own schools of psychotherapy, and watched with disdain the graduate students who had been allowed to attend the workshop in exchange for serving as gophers.

Late in the course of the conference, I was approached by a woman whom I had found intimidating even before I met her. She was famous for her dramatic contributions to therapeutic dreamwork and notorious for her aggressively confrontational style.

When she asked me to help out with the conference she was putting on the following fall, I protested defensively that I was no longer a student and would not make myself available for stuffing envelopes or clerking at registration tables. She laughed at my self-conscious concern and assured me that she'd heard from some of the other senior therapists that I seemed knowledgeable and carried myself well. "I would not ask you to do the dog work," she said. "That we leave to the children."

I was astonished and delighted to discover that instead she was inviting me to act as a moderator. Several well-known painters, composers, and writers were to be paired with appropriate therapists for small-group dialogue. I was to moderate an encounter between a leading art historian and a clinician who had advanced the application of psychoanalysis to group therapy. It promised to be an intriguing interplay of the imagery of a painter facing a blank canvas with thousands of years of art history peering over his shoulder and the concepts of an innovative therapist moving from the turn-of-the-century couch to the contemporary circle of group therapy. With some trepidation, I accepted this delegation of power.

By the time the fall conference was over, I was sufficiently satisfied with how I'd conducted myself as moderator to take my place confidently at one of the lunchtables reserved for presenters and members of the press who were covering the conference. One of the columnists cruelly criticized a playwright at an adjoining table. Because I found his attitude offensive, I took him on. I argued less in terms of theater than in the context of the psychological validity of the playwright's work. Though we contended heatedly for a while, eventually the critic deferred to my authority as a therapist.

During the three-day conference, I spent two nights with a couple of old friends, both of whom were much more cosmopolitan and sophisticated than I. The story I told about my argument at lunch stunned them because they recognized the name of the man I had challenged as a world-renowned theater critic with a reputation for verbal attack that had done lasting damage to people whom he had targeted. If had I known how powerful he was purported to be, I'm sure I would have felt too intimidated to have won out over him.

My ignorance of his reputation for power had afforded me an opportunity to challenge him as an equal. I don't mean to imply that power is only a mirage, or that we can always gain power by a simple shift in perspective. Confidence in our own power can be concretely discredited when we are held captive in the oppressive environments of "total institutions."[1]

I experienced that sort of loss of personal power when I was drafted into the army toward the end of the Korean War. The aim of basic training in a U.S. combat infantry unit is the rapid transformation of a random sample of independent, law-abiding civilians into an army of automatically obedient, professional killers. This corruption of ordinary values cannot be accomplished without first robbing recruits of any sense of being in charge of their own lives.

The deprivation of personal power began insidiously with the stripping away of all emblems of my individual autonomy. My personally selected clothes were replaced with uniforms identical to those of every other recruit, my hair clipped to regulation crew-cut length, and an army serial number substituted for my personal name. That arbitrarily imposed identity was inscribed so indelibly that thirty years later, I remain unable to forget the time when if asked who I was, I automatically answered "US 51257214."

The overriding slogan of the drill instructors was: "Your heart may belong to your mother, but your ass belongs to the Army!" Along with all of the other recruits, I was continuously treated with contempt and kept under constant pressure. We were driven to exhaustion intended to be so excruciating that we would welcome completion of our transformation from civilians into fighting machines.

Although I was never assigned to a combat zone, during those eight long weeks of preparation for battle in an infantry rifleman platoon, I found myself doing things I wouldn't otherwise do—betray other recruits so that they would be blamed for my infractions, malinger to avoid duties that would then fall to my fellow-trainees, and at times engage in fistfights that I thought I'd long ago outgrown when I gave up scuffling in the schoolyard.

Although far less pervasive, the powerlessness endured by draftees is similar in some ways to that induced by persistent stress, deprivation, and selective positive reinforcement of programmed responses imposed in the brainwashing of P.O.W.'s and other captive audiences of programs enforced by the keepers of the keys.

It's upsetting to believe that anyone else has the power to define who we are. We insist, "At times, I may be pressured into acting as if I agree, but no one can tell me who I am or what I believe." Adults confined in prisons, hospitals, or other closed systems, and young children raised in excessively controlling families learn firsthand that these total institutions do indeed define who they are. In such a world, the intrusion of outside power inflicts helplessness so pervasive that its victims are not left anyplace from which to take a safe stand against authority. Instead, they often exercise what little power is left to them in actions destructive to themselves and to others who are even weaker.

People who have been drafted, imprisoned, or hospitalized know what it's like to feel deprived of their independent sense of who they are. If we feel overconfident about our power to maintain our identities in totally controlled institutional environments, we may only add to the danger that they will be defined for us.

By way of example, I will tell you of three young psychologists who were interested in investigating what it would be like to be a patient confined in a psychiatric hospital. They drew lots to select which one would undergo an incognito admission to a mental institution. The psychologist who drew the short straw agreed to apply for voluntary admission to a state hospital where, pretending to be deeply depressed and confused, he was admitted under an assumed name.

When he entered the institution, he was confident that this daring plan would provide the insights that he and his colleagues sought. Within three days of living on the admission ward, the impact of a total institutional setting was so overpowering that this sane, sensible, trusting young psychologist developed the near delusional idea that his two colleagues had tricked him into participating in this project so that they could get him locked up permanently.

Under sufficient duress, there are times when we discover that our *belief in ourselves is more fragile than we would wish.* Confidence in our own judgment can be shaken by situations far less extreme than the tyranny of total institutionalization. Group pressure alone may make us doubt the reality of what we see with our own eyes. I remember how often I questioned my own sanity whenever my mother challenged my non-conformity with the rhetorical question: "Do you *really* believe that the whole world is crazy, and that only you are sane?" It took many years for me to realize that there would be times when my answer might be "Yes!"

A child's sense of power begins with confidence that his mother's authority is benevolent and the feeling that the physical and emotional support he needs are reliably accessible from her.[2] Further development of his sense of power may be arrested at this first stage by the absence of a benevolent mother or by the presence of one who blocks his growth toward more independent sources of strength.

In either case, he will grow up feeling that forces outside himself govern his behavior. Under stress, he is likely to turn to admired authorities, and to depend on alcohol or drugs to enhance his sense of well-being. Influencing others is another way of attaining this feeling of strength and confidence. "The goal of power motivation is to *feel* powerful."[3]

The second developmental stage of a baby's sense of power involves strengthening himself by learning to control his own bodily functions and beginning to say no to the demands of others. This necessary sense of control over his own body and mind makes him feel strong.

Development of the child's feeling of being in charge of himself can be undermined either by a mother who insists on overcontrolling him, or by one who leaves him on his own before he is able to manage for himself. As an adult, his shaky self-confidence will result in perfectionistic striving for self-control, beleaguered by exaggerated distress about occasional failures and inflated upset about external events that disrupt his plans.

Eventually the healthy child reaches a phase when he finds power in competition with others. He learns to feel strong by demonstrating mastery of evolving skills, outdoing other children, exceeding his own past performances, and by making things happen in the world. Aggressive assertion gradually evolves into subtler ways of persuading, bargaining, or maneuvering.

If the child is either overindulged or excessively restricted when he is learning to acquire power by taking on the world, development of his capacity for influencing others can take a negative turn. He may become the sort of adult whose main motivation is to outwit, manipulate, or otherwise defeat other people. Or he may rebel against authority by cutting corners and relying on bragging and deception as the mainstays of his bag of tricks.

If a balance of respectful support and benevolent authority is available to the child, he may then move on to a more advanced stage in which his power begins to come from serving higher principles. He begins to feel good about himself by doing what he believes is right.

This phase is difficult both for the adolescent and for his parents. In the absence of parental tolerance and understanding, the teenager risks mistaking his inflated sense of self for the idealized image of the powers he imagines he is serving. His devotion to higher principles can evolve into self-righteous demagoguery and his doing for others may make him feel like a martyr.

If we are to develop a useful variety of skills and strengths, we must progress through all of these developmental stages. *Power is useless unless it is appropriate to the particular situation in which we find ourselves.* There is an old Chinese saying: "A whale in shallow water amuses the shrimp."

Using the same power mode in every situation results in avoidable failures. A Burmese proverb tells us, "If a needle can pierce it, don't chop it with an ax."

In some situations, *power may provide solutions that are worse than the problem it is intended to solve.* A bit of Yiddish folk wisdom admonishes, "Better a bad peace than a good war."

Some sages say that *in attempting to control others, excessive use of power is likely to ruin what we set out to improve.* The relevant Taoist political guideline is, "Handle a large kingdom with as gentle a touch as if you were cooking a small fish."[4]

4

Power without Purpose

A Sufi story tells of a time when Nasrudin ferried an eminent scholar across a turbulent river.[1] As a way of distracting himself from his fears as they passed through some particularly rough water, the academic pointed out that the ferryman had spoken incorrectly. He asked Nasrudin if he had ever studied grammar. When the mulla replied that he had not, the pedant commented critically, "Then half of your life has been wasted."

Minutes later, the currents grew dangerously stronger. Nasrudin asked his well-educated passenger if he had ever learned to swim. The scholar admitted that indeed he had not. Sighing, Nasrudin answered wryly, "Then *all* of your life has been wasted. The ferryboat is sinking!"

The value of official authority depends on a suitable context. Another Sufi story, in which the wisely foolish mulla is up against a foolishly wise king, suggests that *choosing the wise moment to display power is a matter of perspective.* Because the king enjoyed the challenge of hunting and the company of the mulla equally well, his majesty commanded Nasrudin to join the royal party on a bear hunt. Though the mulla was terrified, he dared not defy the king's command.

When Nasrudin returned to his own village, one of his neighbors asked him about the hunt. The mulla assured him that it had gone marvelously, but when asked how many bears he had seen on the hunt, Nasrudin reported that he hadn't seen any at all. "How could it have gone so marvelously then?" the villager asked. Nasrudin answered, "It was bad enough that I had to obey the king's command to accompany him. When you're me, seeing no bears at all is what makes hunting a marvelous experience."

I've encountered many of these paradoxes in working with my psychotherapy patients. Because I conduct my private practice in Washington, D.C., a fair number of the people who come to me for help about their unhappy private lives are public figures who operate well in the political arena.

Although some of them also appear to function effectively and even creatively in their private lives as well, they often feel empty inside because no amount of success is sufficient to satisfy some unidentified emotional hunger. A patient of mine whom I shall call Paula was one of these publicly powerful people who secretly suffered from inner emptiness. She appeared to operate so effectively that even close friends found it impossible to imagine her hidden suffering, or to consider offering her the sympathy she needed so badly, but for which she could not ask. For a long while, this disparity between her appearance of having it all together and her secret sense of falling apart made it difficult for Paula to seek psychotherapy.

By the time she came to see me, she was suffering from intermittent episodes of uncontrollable sobbing and had no idea why she was so unhappy. Her only explanation for her "crying jags" was to attribute them to her inability to make sense of her occasional, casual sexual affairs with strangers. Paula didn't feel guilty about these encounters, but she was upset about feeling out of control, and feared that her impulsive behavior might jeopardize an otherwise happy marriage and a successful career.

Apart from these isolated problems, she spoke of herself as if she were presenting an impressive resumé at an interview for a high-powered professional position. She spoke of her academic achievements and awards, her doctorate in communications, and her rapid climb up the career ladder. By combining her well-developed social skills with her brilliance and prestigious training, she had rapidly advanced her career in power politics from the municipal to the state level, and then on to national administration, with a reputation for resourcefulness that was becoming international in scope.

Paradoxically, while citing the growing recognition of her achievements, Paula came across as if she was apologizing for herself and expecting criticism from me. When I pointed out how much less impressed with herself she was than her colleagues and her employers appeared to be, she burst into tears. It was the first time she had cried "in front of anyone else" and so she was dreadfully embarrassed.

I told her I felt encouraged by the fact that there

were times when she was unable to keep up a happy face while she was secretly so dissatisfied with her life. It was not what she had expected to be told and she was even more astonished that although I did not necessarily believe that her impulsive affairs were the best solution to her problems, it did seem promising to me that some part of her would not settle for being a good girl who always did the right thing.

I went on to say that something safe and touching about our being together had allowed her to cry openly. In response, she went on sobbing even more deeply for the remainder of the hour.

At the second session, she reported having felt both relieved by my acceptance of her "breaking down" and confused by the fact that I had not admonished her to get herself together and to stop being so "damned self-indulgent." She had chosen to consult me because she'd heard I was tough and confrontational, expecting that I would straighten out her unwarranted "self-sorry silliness" and not let her get away with her ability to manipulate people. For several months and from many perspectives, we examined this theme of her "fraudulent influence over other people." To her surprise, I emphasized her unnecessary sacrifices rather than her unearned rewards.

Gradually, I learned that she'd grown up poor and with little encouragement from her family to attain anything for herself. Her father was an undependable, emotionally aloof alcoholic and her mother a martyred self-proclaimed "wonderful woman" who was never satisfied with anything Paula tried to do to ease her sufferings.

It was not until Paula entered high school that her brilliant resources were recognized. Even then, she remained the misfit adolescent. Because she was smart enough to be teacher's pet, she was unpopular with the other girls.

She identified a second adolescent source of unhappiness when she described herself as having been a "tall awkward, ugly teen-ager with big boobs." Her popularity with boys who were otherwise uninterested in her depended on her being "easy to get for backseat heavy petting."

As a way of escaping her unhappy home, she married early and unhappily, divorced quickly, raised her daughter on her own, and made her way through college and graduate school on scholarships and fellowships. After she attained success as a professional, she made a prestigious marriage to a "wonderful man" who was very different from her unstable father and her unreliable first husband. As I listened to her descriptions of what a sensitive, loving, special sort of man he was, again and again I heard how much like Paula's mother he was in his self-absorption, subtle criticism, and seeming insatiability.

Paula's professional life was an endlessly driven dedication to perfection. She viewed each new achievement as little more than a temporary hedge against her belief that she wasn't a worthwhile person. Nothing she could do was good enough. Whatever she might have accomplished had taken her too long. All of her past work was merely preparation for truly important future projects.

I soon gave up trying to help Paula take herself more seriously and actively devoted myself to joining the resistance. I began by pointing out that she could not be much of a government communications expert because, in spite of her best efforts, nations continue their cold war misunderstandings. I went on to point out that she could not even meddle successfully in the family tangles in her own home.

Paula had unwittingly resumed her childhood role as family peacemaker between her perfectionistic husband and his bewildered teen-age stepdaughter. She insisted on regularly scheduled family conferences in which she tried to serve as mediator. I told her that I hoped that these enterprises were undertaken after dinner, because a family encounter group meeting would take away most people's appetites.

I also pointed out that her husband's self-centered possessiveness and perfectionistic nit-picking were a worthy challenge to someone with her professional training. Having a "practicing paranoid in residence" would keep her on her toes in practicing her communication and mediation skills.

I continued to kid her about her inflated self-serious expectation that everyone was counting on her to set things right in the world. At first she shifted the focus from her "mission" to my "wisdom." Again and again, she would return elated about something I'd said in the previous session that had "transformed" her life.

Each time, I would run it down to get her to recognize that typically my "words of wisdom" were little more than everyday understandings that I was "sometimes" satisfied with myself, that I did my best when I felt like it, and that not everything worth doing was worth doing well. Eventually Paula came to understand that my "powerful" offerings were more often playful than profound. She gradually shed some of her exaggerated sense of responsibility for making everyone else happy and the more she did, the more often we could laugh together.

Paula reported that after she'd been away on a business trip for a week, she returned to discover that her husband and her daughter had settled some of their differences "all by themselves." At our next session, she announced her abdication of being in charge of other people's happiness.

Gradually, Paula's smiling depression decreased, she worked hard less often, and seemed to be having more fun. Despite her fear of her colleagues' envy, she took a more satisfying, less demanding job and was startled to discover not only that many of her co-workers were happy for her, but also that some even felt inspired by her increased freedom.

The job change involved much more travel in the third world, an activity Paula valued most in her career. It meant leaving me before she felt certain that she could maintain her newfound gains on her own. The new job also involved more time apart from her husband, managing her life on her own, and uncertainty as to whether the marriage would endure her autonomy. Paula replaced the power of pleasing others with independence, freedom, adventure, and giving priority to taking charge of her own life. I miss her, but it's hard to imagine that she's not happy.

In the long run, there is no way for anyone to be

totally on top of every aspect of his or her life. Each triumph can make us feel that now we must meet the next challenge even better, transforming each accomplishment into a new obstacle.

It is tempting to become so possessed by the experience of power that we risk violating our personal priorities. By way of example, consider Midas. This ancient, legendary king is said to have captured a satyr in his garden. He treated his captive very well in order to learn his magic powers. The satyr's overlord, Dionysius rewarded Midas by granting the king's wish to have the power to transform anything he touched into gold.

For a time, the king was ecstatic because of the boundless wealth his gift afforded him. He played at turning furniture, plants, and even animals into gold. But then one day, after a long trip abroad, his beloved daughter returned to visit the castle. Midas was so taken with seeing her that he forgot the magic power of his touch, embraced his daughter, and she too turned to gold.

A patient I will call Edward was my Midas. Formally schooled as an attorney, he had used calculated aggressiveness, innovative intelligence, and tactical brilliance to produce a financial empire before he reached the age of forty. His success afforded him all the advantages of wealth and corporate power: luxurious homes and expensive cars, jet-set access to world travel, and political control over institutions, assets, and less powerful individuals. The ups and downs he experienced on his way to the top had never shaken his claimed complete confidence in himself. He was fond of quoting the words of the

Broadway producer Mike Todd: "I've been broke lots of times, but I ain't ever been poor!"

But by the time Edward showed up at my office at age fifty, although not yet a broken man, he was bewildered and unhappy. His devoted wife of many years had threatened to leave him. For a long time she had deferred to him as if he were a god, operating as his informal in-house public relations person and serving as the perfect hostess. She was the jewel in his crown who lavished him with adoration. In turn, he gave her expensive gifts and a life of luxury.

She became whatever Edward wanted her to be and he already was all she had ever wanted. He had made all the big family decisions and she had carried them out without bothering him about the details.

Edward told me that their marital troubles began when he "made the mistake of indulging her whim for a career of her own." Since then she was often not at hand when he needed her, challenged his opinions, and had become "altogether too independent."

He went on to complain that this "menopausal phase" his wife was undergoing was trouble enough. And then their only daughter had "changed from the sunshine of my life to an unmanageable, outspoken, delinquent punkrocker."

When Edward first called me, it was with the idea that he was hiring me to fix his broken wife and child. He had chosen me in particular for the job because they were both "in love" with my books, though he himself had only dipped into my writing here and there, just enough to make sure that I was not "some two-bit guru who might make moonies" of his family.

Edward considered himself "a gray eminence" who influenced financial and political situations both national and international, but his own domestic life was completely out of control. Toward the end of our first hour, I summed this up: "Although you continue to be a very powerful public figure, you're totally helpless at home. The only aspects of your life that you can't manage at all are the ones that matter most to you. It must be confusing for such a big shot to find himself in such a pathetic position."

Edward seemed intrigued by the fact that I did not appear to be intimidated by him. If I'm going to take on a new patient, we usually go to contract by the end of the first hour, but with Edward it took several sessions for him to agree to my stipulations about the frequency and regularity of our appointments, his financial responsibility for missed appointments, and my terms of billpayment and dealings with his health insurance company. He challenged every position I took. Instead of accepting his invitation to argue with him, I simply pointed out how he avoided his discomfort with trust, compliance, and dependency by bullying, extortion, and lawyerly manipulations.

Some of his complaints had less to do with protecting himself from expense and inconvenience than with trying to keep me in an inferior position. For example, he called me a wimp for charging less than the traffic would bear, and a fool for billing by the month when I could have been making more money on fees paid at the end of each hour. I pointed out that paradoxically, in order to gain symbolic domination of our relationship, he wanted me to submit to suggestions that would entail his losing some practical financial advantage. For a long while, he went on insisting that it was stupid of me not to seize opportunities for fair gain. He didn't let up on the issue until after he'd had his staff research the matter deeply enough to discover that my practices were acceptable because they represented "conventional practices" in my field.

Despite Edward's insistence, I did not concur that his wife and child were problems to be solved. His unhappiness had to do with his own attitudes about power, and so I insisted on seeing him in individual psychotherapy. After months of testing out which of us would be boss, Edward begrudgingly accepted that I would remain professionally in charge of the therapy and that he would have to assume personal responsibility for running his life in ways that worked better for him.

Over a period of months, using his part in our relationship as a demonstration screen, together we explored the meaning of Edward's power plays. Gradually, the origins of these dynamics emerged out of remembered and emotionally reexperienced early childhood configurations. From early on, it had been Edward's job to supervise his retarded older brother Willie.

Their mother had to work very hard because their father was passive, depressed, and often unable to earn a living. She "adored" Edward both for his devotion to saving her work, and for being bright enough to control Willie. His father seemed uninterested in anything about my patient except his future earning power. Edward described his parents' mixed marriage as "the unfortunate wedding of a Catholic washing machine to a Jewish financial failure." Since making his fortune, he had a bought a house for his parents and arranged a plan for his retarded brother's lifetime care. He could not hide his prideful pleasure in boasting to me that he had been able to "arrange both ventures as highly profitable tax write-offs."

Once we attained clarity about and some resolution of Edward's own inner personality problems, I suggested that, if it was agreeable to them, he bring his wife and daughter with him for one or more joint sessions. The family session opened with my asking them what it was like living with a character like him. The wife began to complain to me about his overbearing attitudes and emotional inaccessibility, but he quickly cut her off with an angry diatribe about her lack of appreciation of all that he had provided for her.

She looked to me plaintively for protection. In my own paradoxical way, I supported her by asking why she took all this abuse without fighting back. She whimpered some protest of inadequacy. I suggested that she settled for suffering helplessly at her husband's hands just to make him look bad.

At that point, she took him on by telling him that his presents meant much less than his *presence.* As they struggled through this turnabout, for the first time I saw Edward's eyes brim with tears. He was astonished to learn that his importance to his wife was not the strength of his earning power, but depended only on his allowing access to his vulnerable personal self. The thought was almost more than he could take in.

After talking together awhile they turned on their daughter to tell her how worried they were about her having gotten "out of control" by stealing from her employer when Daddy was willing to give her enough money so that she need not have even taken a job. The teen-ager was sullen, saying only that they didn't understand because they never really heard anything she said. Indeed, rather than listening to what their daughter was saying, they drowned her out in a chorus of righteous insistence that their only concern was her happiness, and that what they wanted most was to protect her from getting into any more misbehavior that she would later regret.

I interceded to tell the girl that although I could not guarantee that her parents would really listen, if she wished, I could probably get them to shut up long enough for her to say what was on her mind. She told me she'd like to try. Her parents agreed to try to keep quiet and listen

Even though I had to remind them of their commitment every couple of minutes, the girl had lots to say. She had taken a lousy job because she felt her parents used her financial dependence as a way of controlling her. The boss underpaid her, found fault with everything she did, and had hit on her sexually. Under these oppressive circumstances, she saw her stealing merchandise from him as a perfectly fair exchange.

Both parents seemed astounded. For once, they'd listened to her, but now they did not know what to make of what they'd heard. I interrupted to sum up briefly and point out that they seemed like a family with a lot to work out and some hope of doing so, but that our time was almost up. They wanted more help, and they all wanted it from me. Explaining that my devotion to Edward would make it very difficult to remain a fair witness, I offered to continue my work with him and to refer the wife and daughter to individual therapists of their own. If they wished to continue their joint work, I would also recommend a family therapist who was not seeing any of them individually.

In some ways Edward's family situation reminded me of mistakes I had made with my own children. After struggling for years as an unknown, underpaid staff psychologist at various public institutions and agencies, I had developed a successful and lucrative private practice, and my writings had become widely known. When illness threatened my earning power, I lost hold of my inner power and denied my sense of helplessness by trying to accomplish a great deal in a hurry.

I remember regaining my personal perspective during a particular encounter with my youngest son. It was some time after recovery from my first bout of neurosurgery.[2] My medical future was uncertain and my life expectancy was then believed to be far shorter than it has turned out to be.

Among the many motives for my having written so much was a misplaced attempt to overcome the helplessness I felt about future handicaps and/or early death. I was deeply depressed for a long while partly because like Edward, I believed that if I lost the power to earn a living, along with it I would lose my value to my family. In desperation, I became frantically prolific.

If I learned to write well enough, I could support the family even if I was no longer able to practice psychotherapy, and if the sales of my writings continued, they could be a source of income even after my death. I fantasied myself as a latter-day El Cid. As that medieval Spanish leader lay dying, he asked his aides to tie his dead body onto his horse the next day. In that way, just seeing him at their head, his troops would be led victoriously into battle. I was seeking that same posthumous power of immortality.

One evening while I was writing, my youngest son came into my study to ask to talk with me. At first, I put him off by thoughtlessly telling him that I had no time to talk with him because I was working on a very important chapter. Out of the corner of my eye, I saw his face fall and I suddenly realized that I was trying so hard to control things that I was no longer in charge of my life.

I stopped typing, called him back in, and told him how sorry I was for foolishly forgetting how much I loved him. I don't remember what we talked about, but I'll never forget how good it felt to spend time with him. All at once I realized that, however helpless I might be to control misfortunes such as my illness, I still had the power to take charge of my life by attending to all that mattered most in whatever time I had left to live.

5

Some Stories Have Their Own Power

Radical social-political upheaval reduces otherwise decent people to ruthless seekers of solutions that they would never even consider at times when they feel safe and strong. One shocking example is that of the Ik, a Ugandan hunting and gathering tribe who not long ago were a generous and stable society.[1] The contingencies of African nationalist politics resulted in the arbitrarily forced relocation of these unfortunate people from their familiar and comfortably nourishing hunting ground to a barren, waterless, game-free mountain territory. Government forces transported them to this strange land with the mandate that they remain and become farmers.

The mountain villages to which they were moved turned out to be almost unlivable because the food supply was so limited. Less than three generations later, this punitively barren setting had destroyed the cooperative culture of the Ik. These simple, mutually supportive people became mean-spirited. Love, compassion, and community feeling virtually disappeared. Family life deteriorated to the point where at age three, children were abandoned and forced too fend for themselves.

Hardly any of the displaced Ik survived beyond the age of twenty-five. Those who did were insidiously transformed into devious characters who delighted in sadistic pleasure at the sight of their fellow tribespeople's pain. Older adults were ravaged and deserted by younger, hardier members of the tribe. Grown children often robbed their own fathers and mothers of whatever meager possessions they still had. At times, they could be found forcing half-chewed food from their parents' clenched mouths.

We may be able to understand how the wretched deprivation of the Ik turned them into cruelly desperate survival-seekers. But comparable reactions can occur in far less catastrophic conditions of powerlessness. Helplessness arising out of the experience of seeming abandonment by powerful people on whom we depend can corrupt character so severely that it obscures individual differences in personalities.

During the London Blitz of World War II, to protect the British children against the nightly bombing raids, authorities evacuated many of them from the city. These "infants without families" were relocated in residential nurseries situated in communal foster homes in the surrounding countryside.[2] Most of the children understood that the placement was to be temporary, and that they would be welcome to return to their intact families as soon as it was safe for them to come home.

The group homes into which these preschoolers

were displaced kept them well fed, well clothed, and well housed. Although benevolent institutional supervision was available, the children were deprived of the power of immediate personal access to their own parents. Suffering an experience of life without family and housed with other children whom they had not known, they had to participate in an impersonal competition for the attention of unfamiliar foster parents.

To compensate for the reduction in their personal power, these normally well-behaved children ended up developing delinquent devices for coping with their desperate sense of helplessness. The changes in the children were dramatic and disturbing. Very soon, previously problem-free youngsters displayed uncharacteristic patterns of lying, stealing, fighting, and extortion. They treated other children as a menace against whom desperate defenses had to be mounted.

Even in the absence of identifiable culprits, the immediate and unmanageable suffering of hunger and pain may be morally debilitating. We need not see ourselves as exploited by powerful overlords to be tempted to behave badly. Sometimes, simply feeling powerless is sufficient to subvert our usual standards of behavior.

Although some of us may climb to the top on our own, not many of us are born into positions at the pinnacle of the power pyramid. Most of the world's population remain part of the broad base. Political and economic powerlessness are enough of a problem without the additional burden of the special responsibilities that some subcultures and family systems add to the already heavily loaded backs of the disempowered.

The ethnic insularity of the oppressed encourages emotional extravagance. People who lack objective power subjectively expand the polarities of both resilience and frailty till they seem larger than life. The insistent ability of persecuted minorities to endure oppression is often as astonishing. It is only matched by the debilitation of any actual power to control the oppressive forces with which, if they are to survive, they must learn to cope.

I was raised in a Jewish family. Because of that subculture's passionate romance with words, its members' reactions to persecution are more poignantly stated than those of some other oppressed minorities. In an effort to make some sense of their peculiarly painful predicament, Jews express themselves in an ironic imagery intended as a comic attempt to cope with ongoing misfortune.

A familiar example is the story of a pogrom in which an old and a young Jew were awaiting execution. While the firing squad was being assembled, the younger of the two intended victims whispered to the older man, "I can't stand feeling so nervous. I'm going to ask the guard for a blindfold." The older Jew admonished the frightened younger man, "Shah, don't make trouble!"

It was not until the nineteenth century that Yiddish literature became respectable in its own right. Out of the stories it produced, I will draw on the paradoxical characters that portray archetypal examples of how, even when people lack political power over their external situations, they can remain in charge of their inner selves. These characters represent some of the ways in which members of oppressed communities are able to sustain personal freedom within their souls even while living politically powerless lives.

The wonderfully warm and compassionately colorful Yiddish tales provide a cast of characters who are capable of sustaining the creative tension between being both wise and foolish, courageous and pathetic, melancholy and comical, all at the same time. These portrayals of powerless Yiddish anti-heroes invite both love and laughter. Among others, they include the high-minded, air-headed idealist, the piously luckless loser, and the wise fool, popularly proclaimed the schlemiel.

Surpassing all of the other stock characters of Eastern European segregated Jewish community called the stetl village life is the mensch. No matter how powerlessly embedded in situations sufficiently overwhelming to threaten subjugation of personal identity, the mensch remains a self-respecting person who is committed to maintaining charge of his or her own soul.

The ways in which these fictional characters cope with seemingly overwhelming helplessness provide metaphorical models for our own prospects for retaining self-possesion in the face of powerlessness. They are best portrayed in the touching tales authored by the founding triad of Yiddish literature: Mendele, Peretz, and Sholem Aleichem, and by their contemporary counterpart, Isaac Bashevis Singer.

As a child I was unaware of this literary heritage. When I was young, my mother and father spoke Yiddish occasionally but mainly as one of the many ways in which they maintained their power by excluding me from knowing what was going on. At first they utilized the more common child-rearing practice of spelling out any message that they did not want me to understand. When I grew old enough to learn how to spell, they shifted to using Yiddish for their coded communications. My parents never taught me their private language. I picked up whatever Yiddish I could on my own, solely in the interest of increasing my power to protect myself.

Stories that teach us how to cope with helplessness have their own sort of power. When the original leader of the Hasidic sect saw misfortune threatening the Jews, it was his custom to go into a certain part of the forest to meditate. There he would light a ritual fire, say a special prayer, and the miracle would be accomplished.

When his disciple had occasion to intercede with heaven, long after the leader had died, he too would go to the same place in the forest and say: "Master of the Universe, listen! I do not know how to light the fire, but I am still able to say the prayer." And again the miracle would be accomplished.

Still later, the next generation's leader would go into the forest when it was once more necessary to save his people and say: "I do not know how to light the fire, I do not know the prayer, but I do know the place and this must be sufficient." It was sufficient and the miracle was accomplished.

Several generations later, similar misfortunes needed to be overcome. Sitting in his armchair with his head in his hands, the most recent rabbi spoke to

God saying: "I am unable to light the fire and I do not know the prayer; I cannot even find the place in the forest. All I can do is tell the story, and this must be suffficient." And it was sufficient.

God made man because He loves stories.[3]

6

Rising Above It All

Nobody is exempt from situations in which life seems so out of control that there is nothing we can do to make things right. We all experience occasional helplessness on what we refer to as "just one of those days." First the alarm fails to go off, then there isn't enough hot water to shower off the soap, and next we find that we've run out off coffee. Our bus arrives late and the rest of the day is just one upsetting minor mishap after another. We end up feeling assaulted by chance accidents and attacked by inanimate objects.

When we are lost in temporary lucklessness, fate makes fools of us all and leaves us feeling like powerless victims of inexplicably arbitrary oppression. Battered by one bad break after another, we seem unable to save ourselves. Midway through these dreadful days, we feel like screaming out, "Enough already!" but no one hears our cries. Nobody is there to rescue us from this incessant onslaught of minor misfortunes over which we have no control.

The days of being irritated over trivial troubles seem bad enough at the time, until they pale by comparison at the prospect of crises so serious our lives are threatened to be disrupted completely. Everyone is vulnerable to periods of powerlessness that are later remembered as "the worst times of our lives."

These arbitrary, disruptive episodes occur in many forms and often seem to come in clusters. Things go well for a while. We feel confident and in charge of our lives. Then all at once, the first blow falls, and before we are able to recover our composure, one crisis follows the next. Within a period of weeks, someone we love becomes critically ill, layoffs at work threaten to leave us unemployed, and on top of all that, we learn that our grown child's marriage is breaking up.

During these dreadful onslaughts, much that gives meaning to our lives appears to be in jeopardy. Like a desperately helpless parent passively waiting for an infant's life-threatening fever to break, we suffer circumstances over which we have no control. There is little more that we can do except stand by and hope for better times, foregoing action in favor of patience. While passively waiting, we can only hope that the passing of time will settle the crises we ourselves cannot control.

In the midst of these terrible cycles of calamity, we must sometimes settle for assuming attitudes aimed at making our loss of power more bearable. One of the ways we sometimes assuage our anxiety temporarily is to try to rise above our helplessness by pretending that all is well. Or if our troubles are too trying to be denied, we may insist that if only we maintain the right attitude, somehow we can make things work out well.

Unfortunately, some people assume this comfortingly idyllic attitude to cope with every experience of helplessness. In some situations, they would be better off either facing the pain of their helplessness or, where appropriate, taking action more practically suitable to solving their problems.

Instead, like Mendele's Benjamin, they live a life of lofty illusions.[1] Innocent dreamers believe that right makes might. and that any earnest efforts to rise above powerlessness are certain to get them somewhere. In his satirical novella, *The Travels and Adventures of Benjamin the Third,* Mendele caricatures his anti-hero as this sort of consummate romantic idealist.

Benjamin is a pauper with his poorly shod feet in the mud and his idealistically inflated head in the clouds. With his henpecked neighbor Senderl serving as his Sancho Panza, this Jewish Don Quixote sets out from the village of Tuneyadevka (literally the Town of Emptiness) in a search of the mythical Lost Ten Tribes who he believes have somewhere established a Jewish utopia.

Hoping to leave behind the painful deprivation of extreme poverty and the unrelenting harassment of anti-Semitic prejudices under which he has grown up, Benjamin wanders out into a world on which he has no impact. This air-headed mock-hero becomes a homeless vagrant, pursuing his daydreams. In his absurdly outrageous innocence, Benjamin believes that, simply by speaking rationally in his own enlightened humanism, he can convert any political oppressors and economic exploiters he might meet along the way.

We all know people whose sense of self-importance is as distorted as Benjamin's. Traditionally such people make all the important decisions, such as whether Red China should have a seat in the United Nations, while their spouses decide unimportant issues like what they eat, where they live, and how family matters are to be settled.

Benjamin's self-deception took him and Senderl on a "journey to the uttermost ends of the earth" that predictably got them no farther than the next village. There the two simpletons were forced into the Czarist army.

High-minded but impractical innocence such as Benjamin's is not restricted to the poor. It can also occur in those who have money to spend and freedom to do as they please. Sometimes psychological intimidation is sufficient to keep people from feeling that they can be active agents in the outcome of their lives. There are people politically and economically better off than Benjamin who are victims of family power plays so overwhelming that they end up unable to bear the oppression of their excruciating emotional helplessness. Like Mendele's idealist, some of these people also attempt to transcend struggles that they believe cannot otherwise be mastered.

For example, a patient of mine, whom I will call Joseph, is a bright and charming dreamer, whose own lofty quest is funded by a family inheritance. He came to me seeking psychotherapy because, as he put it: "I'm a promising young filmmaker, but I've been unsuccessful in attaining the ultimate experience that will give my work creative continuity and personal power. Someday my films will offer audiences a vision of the essence of all that is human, but right now, I can't seem to break through the membrane that separates me from everyday reality."

Like Benjamin, Joseph was a world-weary wanderer in innocent pursuit of a noble illusion. He had toured the exotic external world of the Orient, and had explored the intriguing inner space provided by hallucinogenic drugs. Benjamin sought salvation in a religious utopia while Joseph pursued the power of enlightenment by making movies.

He had travelled widely and shot hundreds of hours of film, but seemed as yet unable to edit them down to that aesthetic essence he hoped would someday lift his audiences to higher spiritual planes. In addition to the high-flown frustration, he was also an unhappily isolated and profoundly lonely young man. Opportunities for intimate, long-term relationships came easily, but Joseph moved on impatiently from one friend or lover to another, ever in search of more profound experiences and more perfect mates.

His richly inflated imagination combined with his need to impress me. As a result, he reported many long, lovely, rococo dreams. But no matter how florid his dreams, Joseph always found them unsatisfactory. For instance, if he dreamed he was flying, he complained that a glide path only ten feet off the ground was "tootling" too low to qualify as genuine spiritual or aesthetic ascendency. And when a dream helper appeared to guide him to his destination, Joseph was disappointed if they did not take the "scenic route."

He found therapy equally disappointing, and my guidance too pedestrian. Our conflict came to a head when he came to see me one day complaining on and on about how hard he been working editing a film that had been contracted for production. Bitterly, he contrasted his having to do "exhausting work" with his father's having been a talented artist who performed easily and whom everyone admired. He claimed that his two older brothers both "fell into success," and his mother always derided Joseph as the one boy/man in the family whose limited achievements were worth little because they were extruded out of drudgery, instead of arising out of brilliance.

This meeting took place on a day that had not been good for me. I was coming down with a cold. This discomfort added to the residual pain of an injury resulting from a fall the previous week, and aggravation about ongoing unsuccessful attempts to rectify visual problems left over from earlier surgeries. Additionally, I was writing under the stress of a struggle with a publisher who wanted my book on horror and terror to have an upbeat ending.[2] In response to Joseph's recent frustration about a producer not accepting his latest film-making effort, I shared this experience, as well as my history of earlier manuscripts that were subjected to multiple rejections before being accepted for publication.

Joseph had come to me for sympathy, but I was too fed up to offer anything but an exasperated confrontation about his inflated self-importance, his expectations of instant glory, and his lack of appreciation of how much he had already accomplished so early in his career.

At first, he fought back by emphasizing how easily hurt he was by rejections, both from me and from producers to whom he'd submitted his films. It took a while for him to hear how impressed I was by the beginner's accomplishments of which he made so little, and even longer for him to realize the power he missed out on by comparing himself to people he idealized instead of simply attending to where he'd been, how far he'd come, and where he yet hoped to arrive.

Joseph's aspirations to rise above the problem of powerlessness is one just one variation attempted by the oppressed. Because his head was in the clouds, often he was unappreciative of the impact of the hard won groundwork he begrudgingly undertook. The other accomplished men in the family, and his mother who hungered for immediate gratification, never acknowledged life's everyday difficulties, nor their own frailties.

As a result, Joseph was left feeling inadequate when he had to work hard at something, expecting rewards to come more easily than life usually allows. His family had offered him no model for coping with *faltering and failing, trying again, and then only succeeding at times.*

My own childhood took a turn almost opposite to Joseph's. Although my parents often admonished that, if only I learned to do as I was told I could accomplish anything I attempted, they also insisted I'd never accept the fact that they knew what was best for me. My father worked hard and my mother made sacrifices to give me all that I needed and to inspire my own ambition, but they both made me feel so guilty about their efforts that I began work at age eleven, simply to free myself from the burden imposed by their generosity.

From then on, after school and during Christmas and summer vacations, instead of playing or just hanging out, I worked at delivering grocery orders, loading trucks, waiting tables, operating department store elevators, and clerking in record shops.

As soon as I got my first jobs sweeping floors and running errands for the local grocer and butcher, my mother told me I would soon be fired for laziness and in any case, I would surely squander whatever money I earned. To protect children from being exploited, the municipal Department of Labor required what we called "working papers," job permits that they would not grant to anyone under fifteen. Until they reached that age, kids could only work under informal arrangements with neighborhood shopkeepers. When I was fourteen my mother falsified the date on my birth certificate to help me find a better job.

During too many of my years growing up, I worked when I might have played, believing that money and success were my only hope of attaining the power that would allow me freedom to do as I pleased. Covertly, I countered this dogged industrious by devoting my after-hours time to adolescent delinquencies like petty theft, doing drugs, and playing hooky so I could hang out at the poolroom with assorted unemployed street hustlers.

To my regret, much of my life was misspent in splitting my time and energy between these contradictory alternatives. It took me a long, long time even to begin to understand that work need not be so hard, nor play so risky.

Once I lovingly began to pay careful attention to what made me most happy, I came to realize that freely living my life had nothing to do with whether I was defying or complying with authority. Gradually, I lost in interest in the distinction between work and play and set out instead to take charge of my life by spending as much of my time as possible doing those things that I find personally meaningful, either alone or in the company of people who matter to me.

That inner power has far less to do with pleasing the powerful or impressing the powerless than it does with doing as I please. It depends more on experiencing my input than on displaying my output. I'm learning to work playfully and to play hard. After all these years, I believe I'm beginning to get the hang of it.

7

Polarities of Power in Youth and Age

Joseph's is not the only family pattern that encourages the disempowered child to avoid taking the responsibility for his or her actions. Power struggles pervade the tension between one generation and the next, especially when one parent is sufficiently authoritarian to disavow ever having been a playful child. This undermines respect for the actual child in the family. In response, the other parent will often favor the rejected child.

The child who is unfairly rejected by one parent and overly indulged by the other is likely to remain stubbornly childish in later years, perennially repeating Peter Pan's refrain, "I won't grow up, I won't grow up!"

Paradoxically, an adolescent who is unwilling to accept becoming an adult may later make life commitments as rigid as those against which he or she passively rebelled as a teen-ager. These people are obstinately embedded in passive resistance, just as the parent they once rebelled against was absorbed in tyranny. They often raise their own children in an unintended parody of what they themselves went through. Like the authoritarian parent who rejected them, they unwittingly invite their own mate's overindulgence of the next generation of rebellious children who in turn will also age into authoritarian adults.

This split between tyrannical authority and eternal childishness is in part simply an exaggerated extension of the natural phase-appropriate conflict between generations. Unfortunately when the struggle is intensified by a parent's insistence on overcontrol of the child, it lasts much longer and entails greater emotional costs than the usual adolescent-parental conflicts. The authoritarian parent loses out on the pleasure and revitalization offered by the offspring and the rejected/overindulged youth misses out on opportunities for initiation into the adult community.

The split between the promising youngster and the tiring elder threatens the entire social order by blocking opportunity for succession.[1] The "now scene" of youth appears to exist outside of history. When the new beginning remains in opposition to the old end, there is little hope for an easy transition. A smoother succession of one generation by the next depends on the child's learning from the parent's experience.

While they remain at odds, neither can recognize that the old were once young and that the young will someday be old. Realization may be delayed until the grown child experiences a crisis in midlife. Only then does the aging youth recognize that he or she has become the parent who is now the next to die.

There are positive and negative aspects to both age and youth. The parent is at the same time protector and oppressor of the child. The authority of the parent may keep the child safe, but it is maintained at the cost of restricting the freedom of the young.

The youth feels like an outcast who views the doubts and cautions of the parent as tyrannical pessimism, and the somber concern with day-to-day problems as uncaring coldness. The practical wisdom of age is regarded as compromise, greed, and corruption. In the idealistic eyes of youth, adult life is seen as lacking in passion, hope, and humor—as life hardly worth living.

But for every hopeful youth, dawn inevitably becomes twilight. The once passionate young lover ages into a tired old fogey. Somberly serious and chronically complaining, the senior citizen approaches a second childhood when the infantile self-centered attitudes reappear as full-tilt, know-it-all authority. Destroying what it took a lifetime to build, the aging adult is once again back to wanting only one thing—to get his or her own way.

The fire and passion of youthful exuberance is experienced by the elder as irresponsible impulsiveness and emotional instability. The idealism of adolescence is judged unrealistic and the striving for independence is interpreted as stubborn, negative rebelliousness. Teen-age attempts to inspire and enliven the parents are taken to be disrepectful presumptions. The youth tries out one new project after another, each venture leaving the last uncompleted.

These expressions of curiosity, adventure, and discovery are judged by the elder as the recurrent failures of a kid who just can't stick with anything.

The excited, hopeful adolescent takes on risks that make experience more thrillingly real, while the worldly-wise, fearful parent avoids risks lest they disrupt the illusory, soothing sameness of "the way we've always done things." Youthful innocence needs neither caution nor patience. Living in a perennially timeless state, youth knows only now. Knowing all and needing nothing, the eternal youth is as self-absorbed as the aging authority. As sure of the search for meaning as the parent is of already possessing it, the youth is intoxicated with each new insight and is as dogmatic as as the authority against whom he or she rebels.

In some ways the polarities of power in youth and age are identical. Each is sure of being absolutely right. Both willfully resist change and regard genuine dialogue with the other as contemptible compromise. They cannot come together so long as youth cuts corners and the older generation compulsively insists on doing everything the *right* way. The youth's moodiness is the elder's melancholy, and the spiritual hunger of the one is the materialistic greed of the other. Early restlessness turns into later insecurity and intuitive playing of hunches ends up as inflexible dependence on the tried and true.

The adult who remains overly childlike in character often vacillates between the spiritual commitment typical of youth and fascination with the authority against which he or she continues to rebel. A patient whom I shall call Peter is a clear example of this misguided approach to circumventing powerlessness.

In contrast to Joseph's idealism (see chapter 6), Peter's tricks were sleazy schemes. He dreamily trusted in luck and naive ingenuity as ways of getting what he wanted without having to work for it. Eventually he became addicted to speculation, the easy fix, and the big score to the point where his unrealistic and impractical schemes merely emphasized the pathos of his unfortunate *combining of conceit with gullibility.*

When Peter came to me for therapy he was a boyish thirty-two-year-old high-school guidance counselor hoping to "better define" his life, perhaps even to resume his own education so that he might someday become a psychotherapist.

He opened our first session by announcing that he'd heard I was "the main man, the therapist's therapist, and the daddy of them all." He was certain that I would help him with his emotional problems, and "for the same price" he could learn from me how to do therapy himself. Despite his stated admiration, his contemptuously sardonic smile made it clear that he would never be as "rigid" with *his* patients as he had heard that I was with mine.

During that same initial interview, he labeled himself as a "streetwise hustler and a part-time thief." Curiously, I experienced him as a wide-eyed innocent. His criminal activities turned out to have been restricted to early episodes of unapprehended adolescent shoplifting and current membership in the amoral minority of near daily pot-smokers.

The family pattern that created his youthfully

hopeful character disorder was classic. Peter was the only son of a father whom he described as no fun at all. Boastfully describing himself as playful, flighty, and getting away with doing as little work as possible, he disdainfully categorized his father as a "workaholic drudge" who lacked daring and imagination. I was not surprised when Peter told me that his father disapproved of his son's "free lifestyle" and condemned him as "a lazy hippie with half a haircut."

In a triangulation typical of such authoritarian father/irresponsible son splits, Peter's mother adored her wonder child. At every opportunity she had let him know that he was a very special someone who would never have to worry. She was certain that he would get whatever he wanted badly enough and that everything would turn out just right for him. Though not yet successful at anything that was genuinely important to him, Peter shared his mother's complete confidence that he could "charm" anyone into or out of almost anything.

This manipulativeness was soon tested out in our relationship. He made a case for his special circumstances that he hoped would require my "excusing" him from fulfilling our contract stipulation that he pay for missed appointments just like everyone else. I refused to let him off the hook. He had to make the previously agreed upon payment or I would teminate treatment. I interpreted his acting out this challenge as an attempt to play the *wunderkind* with me as the doting mother. I went on to point out that he was also playing the defiant delinquent against what he imagined was my awesome patriarchal authority which he had initially assigned me.

Except for the contrast with his prior therapist's "lack of integrity," Peter could not quite figure out why my frustratingly unfair insistence on holding him to our contract somehow left him feeling relieved and vaguely affectionate toward me. He wondered if perhaps it was because he felt that I was *not* putting him down. He found it curious that my expectation that he pay his own way made him feel "respected as a man." It was a feeling that he did not yet understand.

Though his good feelings about our relationship were in part genuine, he had a chameleonlike ability to manipulate situations by assuming any position along the power spectrum from obsequious, inadequate servant to spiritual supervisor.

At one point, Peter was certain that he had become my professional protege. He was understandably upset and bewildered when I interpreted this commitment as an oblique expression of secret devotion to the father he held in such disdain. I assured him that his conflict about this allegiance would soon overturn his devoted discipleship to me.

Peter was a quick study. He soon demonstrated the spiteful side of his compliance. Between psychotherapy sessions he signed up for advanced *est* workshop.[2] Although he had attended some of these training seminars between the time that he had left his first therapist and the time that he began working with me, up to that point he had rarely made mention of the experience.

Next time we met, he announced that *est* had

transformed him into his true self He had *"it."* This time he *"really"* had it." He was high on his insights, delighted to discover that "everything is already perfect just as it is!" As a result he was impervious to any interventions on my part. It was clear to him that I too very much needed to attend the *est* workshop. At last he could see that I was attached to a deadly sort of "victim psychology" that mired me in pessimism and kept me attached to past pain and needless suffering. No doubt it was this unenlightened outlook that was destroying my health. It was probably a mistake for him to go on seeing me.

At one level, Peter had learned to protect himself emotionally by yielding to his mother's demands that he be so special that he would never have to earn his own way. Ironically, his careless, lackadaisical, lightweight approach to both study and work also served as spiteful compliance with his father's demeaning discrediting of the worth of any of his son's efforts.

At another level, his mother's vicarious and unrealistically self-centered aspirations for her special child encouraged Peter's fruitlessly idealistic search for an effortless, mystical triumph over life's pedestrian practicalities. He hoped to find a way to stay high all the time, attaining spiritual and emotional growth without any effort on his part.

Because of his need to avoid making mistakes or risking failure, Peter found it hard to dare to try much of anything. Instead, mostly he "hung out and got stoned." Passively waiting to be discovered by the mothers of the world, he rarely attempted to demonstrate his prowess to the fathers.

Chemical intoxicants and their psychosocial equivalents such as *est* simulated the special state his own mother had promised. Once temporarily achieved, these highs tempted Peter to arrogantly authoritarian excesses, equivalent to his father's unwarranted self-seriousness. When Peter was not careless about work and study, he was reckless about play.

Ironically, although *est* is purported to teach participants to give up hope of ever being special, graduates like Peter often end up feeling pretty special once they've "got it!" Before he could do the work that *might* allow him to achieve *some* of what he wished for, Peter would first have to ackowledge his helplessness. That meant making mistakes, extending efforts that did not always pay off, and often giving trial-and-error fumblings priority over inspired intuitive insights.

Peter's patronizing assault on my "unenlightened ego" continued for several sessions and from time to time throughout our relationship, it reappeared. I tried repeatedly to invite his examination of what *he* was doing. The only time my efforts proved effective was when I pointed out that he was sucessfully making me feel the way his authoritarian father had so often made him feel. Eventually his shame at behaving like his hated father began to give way to recognition of his unconscious hope that he could somehow please this man whom he still longed might someday accept him, and whose emotional impact he'd had to learn to defensively discount.

It took many more months of therapy before Peter could see that until he abandoned all hope of

the gratuitously favorable fate promised by his mis-
leadingly indulgent mother, there was no way to get
past the fears instilled by his unpredictable, rage-
filled father. Only then could he recognize *his own*
helpless rage and pent-up grief. Uncomfortably at
first, he began to earn and claim his own power.

For a long time he had viewed me as a curious
combination of wonder-worker and crippled tyrant.
Once open to his tender longings for a loving father
and his wishes for a son of his own to whom he
could pass on the legacy of supported growth from
boy into man, he went on to become a psychotherapist. We were both deeply touched on the day he
said to me, "I used to think you were a powerful and
dangerous magician. Now I can see that there is
nothing that you do as a therapist that I can't learn to
do myself." Then he added, "But I believe I would
like to do it somewhat differently than you do."

Peter had long clung to the illusion that he could
expect to live his life without effort while awaiting
the world's inevitably discovering him and conferring stardom. His change in lifestyle involved the
gradual transformation of this daydream into a plan
that would require putting his powers to practical
advantage. I had to allow the expansion of my
patient's already inflated aspirations for power
before they could contract enough to make room for
his facing the fears that demand attention in dealing
with day-to-day problems.

My task was similar to that of the father who
helped reform his idle sons in an old Sufi story.[3] In
that tale, the sons who had never before listened to
their father gathered attentively around his deathbed

as he told them that there was treasure hidden in the family fields. When he died, they dug up all the fields but found no treasure. Because the soil had already been turned, they decided that they might as well plant some wheat. At harvest time, the crop was abundant. For several seasons the sons repeated this seemingly futile treasure hunt. Though they never did find any gold, these once-passive, failed treasure-seekers became active, successful farmers.

8

Giving In or Fighting Back

Contending with powerlessness can exaggerate people's characters by pressuring their personal style to its extremes. Some people are so humbled by their helplessness that they become accommodatingly unassuming; others are so filled with impotent rage that they live lives of chronic irritability. Either extreme is often taken to the grave, and perhaps beyond.

The caricatured life and death of one particularly unassuming man is portrayed in Peretz's tale of Bontsha the Silent.[1] He died many years ago in a small village in Poland. All his life Bontsha had worked hard as a meek and uncomplaining porter and suffered his misfortunes in silence. When kindness toward others was a possibility, he gave freely but unobtrusively. Although he had accepted help when he was in need, he never demanded it. Silent in life and silent in death, he never spoke a word against God, nor against other people. He died without bothering anyone, going his passive way peacefully and without complaint. At the time, no one seemed to notice his passing. He had called so little attention to his unobtrusive existence, who but God could know whether this simple, uncomplaining man had died of a work-weary broken back or a world-weary broken heart?

When Bontsha died, he was met at the Gates of Heaven by Abraham himself, leading a welcoming assemblage of angels. This modest soul could not believe that their warmth and admiration were meant for him.

They smiled and coaxed him insistently, until in silent bewilderment, he entered the Heavenly Court, fearful that his poorly shod feet might mar the perfect beauty of the gem-studded alabaster floor. It took a great deal of angelic urging to convince Bontsha that the Lord had taken smiling notice of his silent self.

God had issued a Divine Order that Bontsha was to dwell in Heaven for all of Eternity and to be given anything and everything that he desired. Convinced at last, Bontsha smiled shyly and replied, "Well, then, Your Excellency, if that is the Lord's command, could I maybe have each morning a fresh roll and a glass of hot tea?" Hearing his modest wishes, the angels bent their heads in shame.

The death of Bontsha, the silent, was as touchingly unassuming as his life, but not all people are humbled by powerlessness. *The frustration of a life without influence makes some of us arrogant, irritable, and argumentative.* Peretz's Berl the Tailor was such a person.[2]

When he did not show up for services on the high holidays, the rabbi went to Berl's cottage to see what was wrong. The tailor told him that he wanted to register a complaint against the Almighty. Out of pride, he had never accepted charity from anyone, but now he demanded his fair share from God. Otherwise, he threatened never again to go to the synagogue to worship One with whom he had so little influence.

The rabbi tried to argue him into acceding to God's wishes and going to the synagogue, but Berl would not budge. When asked if he would be satisfied if God allowed him to make a decent living, Berl replied, "The devil with livelihood! Livelihood He should have given earlier. I will not serve the Lord again until He agrees, this year, to forgive the sins of man against man."

Although people don't forgive sins easily, God forgives sinners. Because he understood this, the rabbi concurred that if Berl stood fast, he would prevail. With that in mind, the tailor took his prayer shawl and went to the services at the synagogue.

In stories, characters can be typecast as one sort of person or another. In life, people are more likely to be a little bit of this and a little bit of that. We may try to simplify our perspective on ourselves and others, but whatever we might have to say about any person, the opposite is also true. Real-life characters abound in contradictions. The man who has never spoken an unkind word, loses his temper one day and brutally beats his wife. The charitable woman who volunteers as church treasurer turns out to be secretly swindling funds. Others who seem brutally uncaring have been known to risk their own lives to rescue a stranger.

Among my psychotherapy patients, I've never known either a purely innocent Bontsha or an unrepentant, irritable Berl, but I did treat a man I will call Alex who seemed a complicated combination of the two. When we met, he said that reading my writings had made it clear to him that I would be a suitable spiritual mentor to guide him along the arduous path toward fulfilling his career goal. He spent some time elaborating the seriousness and subtlety of his aspirations without ever saying just what it was he wanted to do. Finally I asked him to tell me exactly what he had in mind. Without a hint of irony or humor, he answered simply, "I want to be a saint."

At first I thought that he was kidding, but Alex was dead serious about his vocational ambition. He explained that he had been raised to be the best at whatever he tried. His father had been a high-ranking foreign service officer who demanded top grades and outstanding athletic awards from his only son. He was often away on long, far-off assignments and even when he was at home, he was uninterested in anything other than reports of outstanding achievement. His father's long and frequent absences left Alex dependent on a pietistic mother and grandmother, both of whom insisted on his being "the best-behaved boy in the neighborhood."

For a time, Alex was openly rebellious in dealing with the family pressures for his attaining perfection. He was truant, missed practice often enough to be kicked off the team, and got arrested for minor delinquencies of petty theft and joy-riding. His non-conformity was not so much a reaction to strict demands and arbitrary values, but to the ways they were imposed by his father's aloof, unrewarding attitudes and his mother and grandmother's intrusive surveillance of his every move.

As a high-school teen-ager, he came across Ecclesiastes and remembered it as having changed his life.[3] He went from rebellious truant and mischievous troublemaker to honor role student and valedictorian. Alex made much of the Ecclesiastical preacher's emphasis on the ephemeral nature of all things human and of his admonition that "to every thing there is a season, and a time" for each aspect of life, but oddly enough he seemed to disregard the refrain that "all is vanity." His desire to be a saint seemed mainly an aspiration to elevate himself above other people.

Alex went on to college, majored in comparative religion, and graduated with honors. Next he spent some months as a monastery novice but found the required vow of obedience too stringent for him to stay on to become a monk. Next he went to a Jesuit seminary to study for the Roman Catholic priesthood but could tolerate neither the required celibacy, nor the demands for compliance with dogmatic authority.

By the time he came to me for therapy, he was living a simpler life of service by working as an attendant in an institution for the handicapped. At the same time, he continued his search for a more prominent position by trying to find a way to be ordained as an Episcopal cleric. The diocese had let him assist some in teaching and preaching, but the priest in charge of his church was put off by Alex's arrogant outspokenness.

He presented himself as deeply deferential to both my "professional expertise" and to the "spiritual enlightenment" of my writings, but when I told him that I would see him only if he came at least twice a week, he protested against my "hypocrisy." He accused me of not really caring as much as he did about serving other people, and of trying to control him out of my greed and self-interest.

When I suggested later on that his distrust of my motives could be considered both a way of competing with me for saint-of-the-month and as a way of projecting his own darker side, he was offended and righteously indignant. My seemingly ineffectual interventions were soon confirmed by his having a series of dreams in which a faceless, black-armored knight destroyed those he rode to rescue, and others about bulldozers belonging to "a destruction company," and about "glorious" waves and winds that demolished anything that got in their way. He found his dreams more convincing than my interpetation in persuading him that perhaps he *had* cast me in his own image.

Gradually Alex acknowledged how consciously cunning he could be at times. As he put it, "Words can be dangerous so I choose mine carefully and when I am out of accord with someone, I withdraw into silence, so cold that they get upset and I can blame them for trouble between us."

He was very uncomfortable with this exposure of his less than saintly side. It turned out that his family's righteousness was also fraught with secrets about unacceptable activities. They had stonewalled against any efforts on his part to learn the truth.

There were obscure references to Father's past marriage and children, a history of Mother's hospitalization for what was probably a psychotic episode, and his sister's having undergone an exorcism. Although he sensed the family's dishonesty, Alex was made to feel ashamed for doubting that they were ever anything but the best of people.

The deeper we dug, the more uneasy Alex became about what lay beneath his veneer of perfect purpose and devotion to higher power. Bit by bit, he revealed his fear that beneath his mask of purity was the sinful face of a pervert, an impersonally evil person, or perhaps even a cold-blooded killer. He began to speak of secretly distrusting God and of his long felt fascination with Satanism.

There were occasional hints of hope when he described his thinking as a whore who did not serve truth but was simply the agent of his own secret self-indulgence. In these episodically insightful moments, he was aware that his hidden thoughts and fantasies tyrannized his idealized conscious attitudes. Whenever he was able to stop trying to control both other people's minds and his own, he felt much freer.

Although I saw some movement in our work, I could tell that overall it was not going well. I never knew when Alex was being honest and when he was lying, either to me or to himself. When I confronted him about my mistrust of what he had to say, he seemed temporarily relieved. For a time, he felt reassured that I would not let him get away with hiding his evil secrets, but the feeling of promise did not last. He talked of terminating therapy because of financial problems and of needing more time and energy to devote to spiritual study and service. He subtly suggested that I should do the same, and left.

I had interpreted his wish to leave as an escape from the fearful belief that if he could not appear to be the best of saints, he would be exposed as the the worst of sinners. My own needs for omnipotence became entangled with his and I made the mistake of encouraging him to stay. That made it easier for him to justify his leaving as a necessary avoidance of my satanically tempting him to spiritual corruption.

I should have seen that for everything there was a season, a time for Alex's coming to therapy, a time for his leaving, and perhaps someday, a time for his return. By trying to control the pace of his development, I may have spoiled our chances to accomplish more together. In any case, he left and never returned.

In retrospect, my experience with Alex reminds me of an earlier clinical failure that resulted from my need to believe that nothing was beyond my power. It came at a time many years ago when I worked at a public outpatient clinic at which I often volunteered to take on the most difficult patients, people who most other staff members deliberately avoided.

I decided to work with a young woman I will call Maggie, mainly because I had convinced myself that the other therapists had not chosen to treat her because they were overwhelmed by her physical deformities. My patient was an attractive woman in her early twenties whose birth defects included having no feet and only rudimentary hands. She managed her handicaps with a combination of prosthetic devices and monumental denial.

Like Alex, Maggie had come for help with a vocational problem. She insisted that she would never be happy unless she could become a nightclub singer! By focusing on her frustrated wishes to become a star in the public eye, she avoided her anxiety and despair about the oppressive difficulties of her daily life.

My own parallel defensiveness led me to join in supporting her implausible hopes with denial of my own shame-filled fear of helplessness.[4] Maggie made her own contribution to our helplessness by dismissing my tentative therapeutic interventions. She refused to consider my timid suggestions that her preoccupation with stardom was an avoidance of dealing with the day-to-day quality of her life. Neither of us could face our depression about how badly she had been cheated and how helpless I was to compensate for her losses.

After many despairing weeks of getting nowhere, I turned to a more seasoned staff therapist for help. I told him of my patient's deformities and of her wish to become a nightclub singer. "How can I help her?" I pleaded.

With a wry smile, he answered, "Why not take up the guitar so you can accompany her nightclub act?" At the time I thought his playfully sardonic answer was callous. I was so convinced that I had the power to accomplish whatever was required that I wasn't able to let his helpful irony free me.

9

The Paradox of the Wise Fool

To protect themselves from being pushed around by stronger people, some of those who lack power intentionally play the fool. Their seeming gullibility about what other people tell them is often simulated accommodation aimed at inhibiting the anger of the more aggressive members of the community. Ironically, when they insist on acting so innocent, they invite exploitation and become the butt of everyone else's cruel kidding.

In the subculture of the Jews, this sort of awkwardly innocent, good-natured buffoon is known as a *schlemiel*. In Yiddish literature, Gimpel the Fool is a classic case of this sort of unintended vulnerability.[1]

Orphaned as an infant, Gimpel was taken in, raised, and apprenticed by a baker and his wife. Unfortunately, he was also *taken in* by every bully and wise guy in the village. Because he believed whatever he was told, Gimpel fell victim to one wild put-on after another. Time and again he was sent out to look for evidence of some unlikely event, and then ridiculed for once again having been the butt of some smart-alec's latest prank.

For a long time, he was subjected to trivial mischief-making that left him feeling embarassed when everyone laughed at him. Despite these daily harassments this schlemiel insisted on believing that *"it is better to be a fool all of your life than to be evil for an hour."*

Eventually there came a time when Gimpel became so fed up with this harassment that he talked of moving to another town. Unwilling to lose their appointed village idiot, the local bullies got busy matchmaking a marriage that would keep him around for their entertainment.

They talked him into marrying a local whore named Elka by convincing him that she was a virgin and that her illegitimate son was really her little brother. Elka was an aggressive, loudmouthed liar, but gullible Gimpel was assured that once they married, he would be master of the house and she would become his devoted, loving wife.

She agreed to the marriage on the condition that Gimpel provide a dowry. He gave her all of his savings and arranged the wedding, but he was bewildered that one of the gifts from the village toughs was a crib. When he asked, "Why a crib?' they smirked and told him it might come in handy.

Whenever Gimpel tried to make love to Elka, she always had one excuse or another for refusing his timid advances. He believed whatever she told him and tried not to be a bother. Four months later she gave birth.

When he challenged her, she explained that this was his premature baby. This time, even Gimpel could not believe what he had heard. He asked the village schoolteacher about his bewildering situation and was told that the very same thing had happened to Adam and Eve. According to the Bible, they had gone to bed as a couple and awakened as a family of four.

Gimpel set aside his sorrow, named the child for his father, and devoted himself to working even harder to feed the baby, his wife, and her little brother. As a result, he had to sleep at the bakery all during the week and when he returned home on Friday nights Elka always had heartburn, a headache, hiccups, or some other excuse for not sleeping with him. Gimpel accepted his deprivation in silence, saying to himself only, "What's one to do? Shoulders are from God, and burdens too."

One night, the oven at the bakery burst and Gimpel was sent home early. Arriving unexpectedly, he heard two snores coming from his wife's bed and saw that a man lay next to her. Fearing that he might wake the baby, he tiptoed out. When he got back to the bakery, he decided that he had been a jackass too long and said to himself, "Gimpel isn't going to be a sucker all his life. There's a limit even to the foolishness of a fool like Gimpel."

The next morning, he went to the rabbi for advice and was told to divorce Elka. Gimpel agreed, but by nightfall he longed to see his wife and child again.

He didn't have it in him to be really angry and so began to make excuses for Elka. Gimpel talked himself into believing that because he had not spent more time at home and had provided so little financial support, his wife's vulnerability to the bribery of gifts and seduction by a stranger was vindicated. But no matter how hard he tried, even Gimpel could not accept such outlandish rationalizations. Instead he decided that he must have been mistaken about seeing the stranger in his bed because, after all, "hallucinations do happen."

He returned to the rabbi's house to confess his error. It took the rabbinical council nine months to come to an agreement about this confusing matter, and by then Elka had given birth to yet another child, this time a girl who Gimpel named for his dead mother-in-law.

As usual the villagers enjoyed themselves at Gimpel's expense, but he resolved to go on believing what he was told. "What's the good of not believing? Today it's your wife you don't believe; tomorrow it's God Himself you won't take stock in."

By then Gimpel was a full-fledged baker with an apprentice of his own. Each day he sent the young man to take food to their house for Elka and the children. One afternoon when Gimpel too went home, he discovered the apprentice in bed with his wife.

Elka sent Gimpel to the barn, ostensibly to check on a sick goat. When he returned, the young man had vanished. She assured her foolish husband that an evil spirit had dazzled his sight. The next morning when he checked out his experience against the apprentice's denial, the young man convinced him to go see a doctor to heal his ailing mind.

During the twenty years that Gimpel lived with his wife, she bore six children. He went on believing what he was told "because a good man lives by faith." On her deathbed, Elka begged Gimpel's forgiveness for having deceived him. He forgave her for her deception, but could not forgive himself for having been such a fool.

When the period of mourning was over, the devil came to Gimpel in a dream and told him that because the whole village had deceived him, he ought to deceive them in turn. The Evil One suggested that each day Gimpel should accumulate a bucket of urine, pour it into the dough each night, and trick his enemies into eating loaves contaminated with filth. Although it was tempting to take vengeance against his oppressors, Gimpel hesitated because he was worried about how he would be judged in the world to come.

The devil assured him that there was no Heaven and no God and that Gimpel's unwarranted worry was only the outcome of his having been sold yet another bill of goods. Gullible once again, Gimpel set out to do as he was told. At the last moment, he realized that like his wife, the villagers had hurt no one but themselves. He took the hot loaves out of the oven and buried them in the yard behind the bakery.

Gimpel gathered up what little money he had, gave it to his family, and left town to wander with his beggar's sack telling stories to children he met along the way. Like Gimpel, they too were willing to believe whatever they heard and so he made sure he never told them anything that might do them harm. With his own gullibility transformed into faith, he someday hoped to arrive in Heaven. "Whatever may be there," he believed, "it will be real, without complication, without ridicule, without deception."

God be praised: there even Gimpel cannot be deceived."

There are times when we feel so helpless that anyone of us may be tempted to trust and depend on people who seem more powerful than we are. We look to experts, authorities, caretakers, and sometimes to *almost anyone other than ourselves* to tell us what's what and what we should do next. During these trying times, it may be difficult to remember that, however powerful anyone else might seem at the moment, there will be times when even the most mighty make mistakes, feel overwhelmed, and fail. Eventually everyone dies. Just like Life, Death makes fools of us all. <u>None of us can afford to miss the opportunities for freedom to be in charge of ourselves and to laugh and enjoy what we can.</u> Retaining this faith is what makes us more than simple fools.

No matter how powerful a person may be, each has his or her own frailties. There will always be some things beyond our control. Embarrassment is inevitable from time to time. Situations arise for which we simply are unprepared. *However well we may prepare, the moment belongs to God.* At times, circumstance demands more of us than we had anticipated. <u>In other instances we cannot cope simply because too much has been expected of us.</u>

We experience these discrepancies as embarrassment. Normal people in everyday social situations react this way involuntarily. Anyone caught off balance is uneasy— not because the person is maladjusted, but rather because he or she is not.

Embarrassment is *not* a personal flaw. On the

True:
    Even if <u>we</u> have contrived the expectations.

contrary, it is a useful transitional pattern that allows us time to reestablish more orderly, adequate behavior. The flustered person unwittingly reveals his or her responsiveness to the discrepancy between expected and actual performance. Perceiving this uneasiness, other people are in a position to help reestablish the earlier state of unself-conscious ease and the blunderer can regain his or her sense of inner power.

Because we live with idealized goals of what we should be, we are sometimes subject to feelings of inferiority. Even these momentary discomforts can serve us well by establishing attainable future goals that someday will bring new rewards and pleasures to our lives. *Everyone has dreams of triumph and fantasies of humiliation.*

If we have not been subjected to excessive shaming, *failure may be experienced as no more than not yet attaining what we might.* People who have been made to feel worthless too often experience each failed attempt as if it implied that they themselves were total failures.

There is no way for anyone to avoid ever playing the fool. None of us is sufficiently wise, competent, or consistent to escape ever making a mistake, failing, or acting just plain silly. From time to time, we must each endure the periodic embarrassment of helplessness.

I no longer ask myself, "How can I get past playing the fool, once and for all?" Instead I ask "How can I learn to go through these inevitable episodes of embarrassment without feeling needless shame?"

I'd like to learn to accept more fully my sometimes foolish Self, to be more true to my natural foolishness, to know better how to enjoy it all. If I must sometimes be a fool, at least let me be a *wise fool.*

The fool played only a minor role in the European literature of the Middle Ages until Erasmus wrote *In Praise of Folly*, and gave the West *the paradox of the wise fool.*[2] In the Renaissance, the fool stepped forward as a major figure in the humanist vision. Erasmus' wise fool continues to foster self-acceptance.

His book is a work of great irony, delicately balancing the comic and the serious in the proportions necessary to get through a life in which we are at the same time both earnestly powerful and absurdly powerless. Folly herself delivers the discourse as she satirically challenges the wisdom of the powerful princes, clergy, and academics of her time. At the same time, she boasts of her own failings and frailties, lovingly contemplating her weaknesses as though they were strengths. Like Socrates, her only claim to wisdom is that she knows that she knows not.

Like so many later fools—Don Quixote, Huck Finn, Chaplin's little tramp, and the Marx Brothers,— she does not comprehend what society expects of her. Like all clowns, she is free to walk irreverently through the walls of convention simply because she does not see that they exist. Often enough these hollow boundaries collapse before the force of her seeming ignorance.

Fools rush in where angels fear to tread. The good judgment attributed to those in authority is sometimes no more than the closed mindedness of people presumed to know better simply because they run things. Folly challenges this presumption, saying:

> If prudence depends on experience of affairs, to whom does the honor of this attribute belong? To the wise man, who, by reason of modesty and partly of faint-heartedness, will attempt no action? Or to the fool, who is not deterred from any enterprise by modesty, of which he is innocent, or by peril, which he never pauses to weigh? The wise man runs to books of the ancients and learns from them a merely verbal shrewdness. The fool arrives at true prudence by addressing himself at once to the business and taking his chances.[3]

By accepting the fool in myself, I open my imagination to all the possibilities that I was once too wise to consider. Shamelessness frees us to dare anything! To gain real wisdom, we need only be sufficiently brazen to persist in boldly playing the fool. If only we recognize the universality of the fool in everyone, regardless of the inequitable distribution of other strengths and weakness, Folly has the power to destroy many illusions.

Accepting myself as a fool tears the cobwebs of conventional wisdom from my eyes and offers me a powerful place of my own. After all, "a normal, reasonable man is expected to 'know better' than to criticize the accepted order of things but the fool is not expected to *know* anything. He is a difficult adversary to combat, precisely because he is only a fool."[4]

When I was young I hoped to make fewer and fewer mistakes. Now my ambition is to make more.

I want to sin boldly. I still dislike being embarrassed, but if feeling foolish is the price of trying out unorthodox ideas and unauthorized actions, much of the time that helplessness seems worthwhile.

I have succeeded in making more mistakes now than when I was young. In part, that is simply because I now risk imagining the unthinkable, saying the unspeakable, and doing the unacceptable. As a result, in these later years, I am wrong and fail more often, but I am also right and succeed more often. My most recent mistakes are more likely to be sins of commission than of omission.

I relish advertising myself as an eccentric anarchist. As an oddball, I am not expected to behave myself, nor am I bound by traditional social values. This shift from external rules to inner guidelines redefines all principles in accordance with my own personal perspectives.

Zen Buddhists encourage acceptance of human frailty by pointing out that "a petty fool is nothing but a worldling, but a great fool is a Buddha."[5] Many Zen masters are clowns, the studying of koans (riddles in the form of a paradox) is a comedy of errors, and enlightenment often occurs in an outburst of hearty laughter.

My own favorites among these gurus have "the appearance of tramps, the demeanor of madmen, and the comportment of pranksters." Even at the point of death these wise fools remained irreverent spiritual clowns. A classic instance is the deathbed dialogue between an eighth century Zen monk named Teng Yin-feng and his disciples.

The dying master said, "I have seen monks die

sitting and lying, but have any died standing?" "Yes, some," was the reply. But he went on to ask, "How about upside-down?" they answered, "Never have we seen such a thing!"

Whereupon Teng stood on his head and died.

To the wonder of those who came to view the remains and the consternation of those who had to dispose of them, when it was time to carry him to the funeral pyre, Teng remained upside down. Finally, his younger sister who was a nun came, and grumbled at him, "When you were alive, you took no notice of laws and customs, and even now that you are dead you are making a nuisance of yourself."

The Taoist clown/priests also insisted that even at the grave time of death, conventional wisdom and rules of conduct must not be taken too seriously. When Chuang Tzu discovered that his disciples were planning a splendid funeral for him, he demanded to know why they were wasting all that effort when they knew that if he went unburied, he would have all of heaven and earth, the stars and the planets about him.

His disciples protested that if he remained above ground, he would surely be eaten by crows. The Master of the Tao replied, "Well, above ground I shall be eaten by crows and below it by ants and worms. In either case I shall be eaten. Why are you so partial to birds?"

By playing the clown and the fool, Oriental teachers refused to put themselves above other men. They encouraged a fellow-feeling of fools among the community of ordinary people. *Nothing was too sacred to be laughed at.*

Reason, hierarchies, and all other distinctions were overturned by these great levelers. They were wise fools for whom no category was too important to be made fun of by standing it on its head. Their grand folly turned out to be an acceptance of everything just as it was, laughter that liberated, and the celebration of human imperfections. They made no distinctions between the sacred and the comic, the sublime and the ridiculous, or the rulers and the followers. By taking things as they are rather than as they should be, they encouraged inner power and freedom for all of us to laugh at our own follies and frailties.

10

In Charge of One's Self

What's an ordinary person to do? If we're poor and oppressed, how are we to make our way? How can we learn to cope with things we cannot change, and what will it cost us to try? The characters in Yiddish literature offer several prototypes for solving these problems, but so far, each solution poses its own problems.

The inflated idealism that allowed Mendele's Benjamin to rise above feeling helpless left him out of touch with everyday realities. The uncomplaining submission that   obscured the deprivation suffered by Peretz's Bontsha demanded the total sacrifice of his personal self. And while Berl's arrogant insistence that he shouldn't have to put up with a life that is so patently unfair allowed him to indulge in the spiteful satisfaction of not cooperating with those who wielded power, in the end his stubborn holdout amounted to little more than chronic irritability. Singer's Gimpel's seemingly good-humored attitude of passive resistance resulted in his playing the fool more often than he might have.

Now let us look at Sholem Aleichem's Tevye, the most human and universally appealing of Yiddish literary characters.[1] Tevye is the archetypal *mensch,* a powerless folk hero sufficiently in charge of himself to be *a victim of oppression who prevails as a person in his own right.* Because he is a mensch, Tevye endures with dignity all that must be suffered and complains only as much as each calamity absolutely demands. Occasionally, he can be heard crying out: "Dear God, it's true that we are the Chosen People. But once in a while can't You choose someone else?" Even in the midst of misfortune he remains a decent, responsible, and caring person who refuses to use the unfairness of life as an excuse for behaving badly toward those less fortunate than himself. By balancing the tenderness of his heart against the harshness of life, he continues to try to make his way as a just man in an unjust world.

Although misfortune may rob him of everything else, he is able to retain both his self-respect and his sense of humor. As Tevye puts it in one of his frequent comments to the Almighty: "As the Good Book says, 'Heal us, O Lord, and we shall be healed.' In other words, send us the cure, we've got the sickness already. I'm not really complaining—after all, with Your help, I'm starving to death—three times a day, not counting supper. You made many, many poor people. I realize, of course, that it's no shame to be poor, but it's no great honor either." Letting up a little on the Lord, Tevye goes on to say, "We don't really starve, but we don't eat like kings either.

When a poor man eats a chicken, one of them is sick."

Tevye is an incarnation of the traditional culture of the Eastern European shtetl culture where "life is with people."[2] In the shtetl, everyone suffers both economic poverty and political oppression. The only hope for these powerless people is their devotion to keeping the faith, but even this is not a matter of blind obedience for no leader has absolute authority, not even God. The Lord may have made the laws, but it is up to the people to figure out what He meant by them. The letter of the law is not the crucial issue. It is the spirit of the law that counts to them, and that can be determined only by how it affects people's feelings and their sense of well-being.

Whatever little power a stetl Jew might have is never to be abused, no matter what the circumstances. Frequent quarreling is acceptable, but it is considered beyond the bounds of decency to take advantage of another person's true vulnerability and to inflict real shame. During an argument, a mensch is free to denounce an adversary "for any or every sin you can think of, but refrain from mentioning the one thing that would bring the flush of serious shame to his or her cheeks."[3]

A stetl Jew can curse an adversary imaginatively and outrageously by saying such things as, "You should lose all your teeth but one and in that one, you should have a toothache!" But no matter how agitated one gets in a personal power struggle, it is not permitted to bring up the one thing that would hurt most, such as knowledge that your antagonist's spouse is suspected of infidelity.

The admonition: *"Be a mensch!"* means "act like a *person,"* in the best sense of that word. This is not as simple as it sounds. Integrity has nothing to do with success, nor with wealth or social status. Every person must be judged on—and only on—his or her merits, judged openly and without prejudice. Yet, at the same time the mensch is committed to respectful acceptance of the other's point of view in a confirmation that must be offered without compromising or betraying his or her own integrity.

To remain in charge of their own lives during this immersion in the paradox of blessed disempowerment, the stetl Jews had to sustain both self-reliance and a generosity of spirit toward other powerless people. The creative tension between these seemingly antagonistic attitudes is touchingly conveyed in the traditional questions:

"If I am not for myself, who will be for me?
And if I am for myself only, what am I?" [4]

Tevye lived and worked as a weary dairyman. He and his wife were already poor and had the additional burden of several daughters whom they had to marry off. Ironically, it was these dearly loved daughters who challenged Tevye's traditions. Out of respect for their individual freedom, he had taught them to stand up for what they believed in. Like many supportive parents, he had not imagined that someday the autonomy he had instilled in them would be asserted against him. Each of his daughters was a mensch in her own right.

Each fell in love with or married a man who represented a break with stetl tradition. Rather than accept an arranged match that would offer financial advantage to the family, the eldest daughter, Tsaytl, simply wanted to marry for love. Although Tevye was offended by this assault on the stetl tradition of parental authority, not only did he put Tsaytl's happiness first and endorse the match, he also went on to see the young couple through hard times.

Another daughter, Hodl, followed her lover into the Russian revolutionary movement. It was a time when many young Jews defected from their parents' seemingly impotent orthodox religious beliefs to the promise of overthrowing oppressors by political action. Tevye was frightened and bewildered, but he saw Hodl off and wished her well.

A third daughter, Chava, wanted to marry a Gentile. Tevye struggled to make peace with his helplessness in this arena as well, but it was more than his conscience could allow. When Chava pleaded with him to accept their marriage, Tevye let out another anguished outcry to God, saying, "Accept them? How can I accept them! Can I deny everything I believe in? On the other hand, can I deny my own child? On the other hand, how can I turn my back on my faith, my people? If I try to bend that far, I will break. On the other hand there is no other hand. No— no— no—!"

As you can see, being a mensch is no easy task. Faced with tides he could not stem, again and again Tevye had to choose between trying to control other people and simply sustaining his integrity by remaining in charge of himself.

Like Tevye, some of my patients are not only able to survive oppressive personal histories, but to prevail against awful odds. The joyful astonishment of watching these people blossom is reminiscent of times when as a child wandering the mean streets of New York City I came upon a wildflower stubbornly emerging out of a crack in the sidewalk. My work with such patients is less a matter of assisting their drive toward self-improvement than supporting their uncertain self-acceptance, helping them to get out of their own way, and watching with wonder as their inner power comes into full flower.

A patient I will call Vincent clearly demonstrates this power of the human spirit to survive conditions that could easily have beaten it into submission. He was raised in a physically brutal and emotionally barren environment where he protected himself as best he could, took nourishment where he could find it, and ended up a more decent and developed human being than many people more advantaged than himself.

Vincent grew up in the sort of impoverished neighborhood where most kids were more likely to do time in jail than to finish high school. His father was an abusive alcoholic who bolstered his own battered self-esteem by wielding the inflated patriarchal power of beating his sons and molesting his daughters.

Although Vincent's mother was kinder, she rarely attended to the children's feelings about what they wanted for themselves. Instead she intrusively pushed them to achieve whatever she felt would demonstrate to the neighbors that she was a good mother. Her forced feeding kept them overweight, and her pushy ambitions required their sacrificing play-time to unwanted afterschool lessons and prolonged practice of arts that thcy hated. By the time Vincent was ten, his mother had died, leaving her overburdened husband drinking more heavily and behaving more irresponsibly.

Vincent and his older brother bonded together as jesters who mocked the tyrannical abuse of their father's authority, and as mischievous pranksters who acted out playful parodies of the demanding aspirations imposed by their mother. An immigrant maternal grandfather was another source of emotional support for Vincent, both in his love for his grandson and in his traditionally feelingful old country ways.

By the time Vincent came to me, he was a happily married man in his thirties who dabbled in art, magic, and music, while working hard at completing a graduate program in psychology. His presenting problems included concern about overeating, occasionally drinking too much, and often driving dangerously.

As I got to know him better, he also revealed that he thought of himself as a shallow trickster. Although his dazzling displays of talent entertained his audiences, Vincent feared that he would never follow through on any project of substance.

Before we ever met, he had read some of my writings and developed the fantasy that I was a benevolent master who would pass my power on to him by revealing my secret mystical wisdom and conferring my blessing. As he got to know me, a darker idealization evolved. He took my wearing black motorcycle boots to mean that I had once been a renegade biker and a deadly street fighter. He imagined that the pendants I wear indicated that by now, I had risen from the rank of Mafia soldier to become the Godfather whose legacy I might bestow on him.

For many months, Vincent invited me to play a variety of power games with him. First, he attempted to undermine my authority by trying to entice me to collude in defrauding his health insurance company, but when I refused he seemed relieved to learn that I was "incorruptible."

His efforts to discredit his own integrity also took the form of missing appointments, paying late, and mailing me a check that bounced. Vincent was certain that, no matter how impressed I might have been with him at first, eventually I would recognize that he was "really a fake and a fuck-up" whom I would be forced to "expel because of incorrigible misbehavior."

As the acting out of his power plays yielded to my interpretations, Vincent delved deeper into his secret self. His heroic dreams and fantasies included images of manning a machine gun at a gateway through which hordes of evil forces attempted to invade. At first, these assaults always ended up with Vincent's getting killed while taking down as many bad guys as he could in his attempt to save the children and comrades he was committed to protect.

Beneath his impotent rage was an underlay of soft and sensitive vulnerability. When his hidden grief gradually began to emerge, Vincent visited the cemetery where his long dead mother was buried. I was touched when he told me about kneeling at her graveside where to his astonishment, he found himself asking aloud, "Mom, did I turn out all right?" and then unexpectedly sobbing.

Later, his powerfully assaultive father was incapacitated by a stroke. All through their battered childhood, Vincent and his brother had daydreamed of the time when the old man would one day become weak enough to be a target for their vengeance. But when that time finally came, Vincent recognized that his father had been no more than a carrier of a generations-old family pattern of abuse, a burden Vincent was grateful that he himself had been able to put down.

Once he had gotten beyond trying to control me, Vincent began spending his therapy hours lying down with his eyes closed and his attention directed to taking charge of his primary quest, the discovery of his own inner power. During those explorations, there were times when he felt helplessly empty and would ask me to teach him how to acquire the wisdom and power he attributed to me.

One time, I responded by telling him the story of the members of a Hasidic congregation who had become helplessly lost in a dense forest. They were delighted when unexpectedly they came upon their rabbi who was also wandering through the woods. They implored, "Master, we are lost! Please show us the way out of the forest."

The Rabbi replied, "I do not know the way out either, but I do know which paths lead nowhere. I will show you the ways that won't work, and then perhaps together we can discover the ones that do."

Gradually giving up his need to impress other people allowed Vincent to pay increasing attention to taking charge of himself. When he was leaving a position on a clinic staff to go into private practice, his preoccupation with whether his colleagues would miss him suddenly shifted to how much he would miss them. He had begun to enjoy the poignancy of *the inner power that arises out of loving others rather than being loved by them.*

The focus of his professional development shifted as well. Vincent became able to stick to reading complicated clinical material without suffering his earlier premature loss of interest. He began to read for intuitive understanding that would broaden his outlook and add to his inner power, rather than for memorization aimed at an outward display of mastery that could be performed on demand.

When he no longer had to see himself as a total failure, he felt freer to to try out new ways of working that he knew would sometimes fail. By the end of therapy, he had given up the idea that I would anoint him, and boldly told me, "I'm learning to do all the things you do as a therapist, but I'm changing them in ways that work better for me."

He had begun making choices that suited his beliefs and principles, regardless of their popularity or unpopularity. His increased self-acceptance replaced the secretly superior perfectionism that had so often made him feel needlessly inadequate. As his transformation allowed him to replace his earlier competitive self-comparisons with more genuine involvement with other people, he lost interest in his chronic concern with judging who was right and who was wrong.

Although Vincent remained generous, after

years of giving exorbitant gifts to others, he felt freer to satisfy his own needs in ways he had once felt he was unworthy of deserving. The recurrent, exhausting dreams about renovating houses with impressive facades that he had reported during the early part of the therapy began to be replaced by exciting dreams of exploring homes where he discovered hidden rooms filled with enough unexpected treasures for everyone to have a share.

He felt freer to say no to friends when he really didn't want to respond to their requests and for the first time, was able to give anonymously with less interest in receiving other people's gratitude than in enjoying their pleasure. Vincent also began to take better care of himself by more often eating and drinking only as much as he wanted, and by driving more sensibly.

When we first met, Vincent had felt ashamed of his "lower class, blue-collar" background. He was often awkward and self-conscious about having what he termed "the appearance, manners, and sense of humor of a truckdriver." As his inner power evolved, he began to appreciate the authentic earthiness of his personal style as a rich and colorful heritage, well worth cultivating, rather than as a rough, wild undergrowth that needed weeding out.

His growing autonomy as a mensch allowed him to distinguish better between manners and morals, between personal, social, and political issues, and between pride and principle. He became less patronizing and more patient with human frailty, both in himself and in other people. As his need for controlling the outcome of his actions diminished, he felt freer to risk going the distance, even when he knew that he might fail.

Near the end of his therapy, he told me a baseball story about three home-plate umpires who were comparing how each approached his work. It was Vincent's way of describing the stages of personal development he had moved through as a psychotherapy patient.

The rookie umpire said, "I calls 'em as I sees 'em." The one who was somewhat more experienced said, "I sees 'em as I calls 'em." The veteran umpire said, "Until I calls 'em, there ain't nothing to see."

The archetype of the mensch that had become so central to Vincent's life is touchingly expressed in an old Jewish legend of the Lamed-Vov. These thirty-six hidden saints were known as the Just Men. Their mission was to roam the earth caring about human suffering, while knowing they could do nothing to relieve it. Traditionally, it was believed that so long as the heartbreaking depth of their caring went on, God would allow the world of ordinary people to continue to exist.

Each of these just men had his own singularly personal way of hallowing everyday experiences in the community. Rather than teach doctrine, each one demonstrated a way of life in which the most important thing was whatever he happened to be doing at the moment.

When his disciples complained about how different he was from his predecessor, one of the Lamed-Vov replied, "We are just the same. He did not imitate, and I don't either."

When another of these hidden saints was challenged about living his life his own way, he responded, "When I get to the gates of Heaven, I will not be asked, 'Why were you not more like your teacher?' but, 'Why were you not more like yourself?'"

Like Vincent, I try to live life as a mensch as much as possible—sometimes more, sometimes less. I am no Lamed-Vov, no hidden saint, but I do what I can.

My anguish is more for my own place in this world than for humankind's lot. I identify most easily with that Just Man who started out for Sodom, hoping to save its people from sin and punishment.[5] He preached in the streets, crying out to the sinners and urging them to change their ways. Although no one listened and no one responded, he went on shouting his message of warning and his promise of redemption.

One day a child stopped him and asked why he continued crying out knowing that he had no chance of ever being heard. The Just Man answered, "When I first came to Sodom, I shouted my message hoping to change these people. Now that I know that I cannot change them, when I cry out it is only my way of preventing them from changing me."

And so it is with me as well. I don't do psychotherapy to rescue others from their craziness, but to preserve what's left of my own sanity. And my writing is less a way of teaching others what I know than of reminding myself to remember what little I have learned about being a mensch.

11

Release from Domination

We need not remain stuck in a subordinate position simply because someone else appears to have the upper hand. This paradox is inherent in the nature of power and freedom, and it is demonstrated exquisitely in Dostoevsky's parable of the Grand Inquisitor. [1] In this wonderfully instructive interplay of the forces of good and evil, Christ was held captive by order of the Church. The Grand Inquisitor entered the dark cell to accuse Him of having offered the people *both authority and freedom.*

Because the Inquisitor believed that ordinary human beings are no more than evil, undisciplined animals, he insisted that this paradox could not be allowed to remain unresolved. The Church of the Inquisition had set out to correct Christ's error of having set people free to sin. He insisted that *for their own good,* the Church must maintain unquestioned, repressive control over them.

The Inquisitor admonished his prisoner for having set a bad example of authority for humankind during the forty days in the wilderness where Satan had thrice tempted Him to display his power.[2] The first time, Jesus had refused to appease His hunger by performing a miracle of making bread out of a stone; He would not offer people material security as a reward for accepting His authority and instead had insisted that "man shall not live by bread alone."

Next, in exchange for His willingness to worship Satan, the Evil One had offered Him immediate power over all the kingdoms of the world. Jesus would not agree that authority must be obeyed whether it was good or evil, and so He replied, "Get thee behind me Satan: for it is written, Thou shalt worship the Lord thy God, and him only shalt thou serve."

Finally, Satan had set Christ at the top of the temple in Jerusalem and urged Him to cast Himself down, promising that the miracle of His being saved by angels would assure complete control over those who worshiped. Jesus answered, "Thou shalt not tempt the Lord thy God."

Refusing three temptations to control people by deceiving them, Jesus affirmed that people must decide whether or not to follow Him by their own free choice. The Inquisitor argued that all of these decisions were unsuitable acts of misguided authority for which the Church would punish Him.

Throughout all of the Grand Inquisitor's threatening accusations and angry arguments, Jesus sat in silence and did not attempt to defend Himself. At the end of the long harangue, He kissed the Grand Inquisitor gently on the lips. The authoritarian oppressor was so moved by the way in which Christ had redefined their relationship that he opened the cell door and set Him free.

The reciprocal roles of dominance and submission are *not necessarily* determined by one person being stronger than the other. In situations where two people have equal power, the one who lets the other get away with *defining the relationship* is likely to end up feeling helplessly oppressed.

A clear example would be an argument in which one person implies, "If you don't agree with what I say, there's no point in my going on talking with you." Ordinarily, this simple sort of threat is no more than a straightforward attempt at intimidation. To defuse the imposed authority, all the designated subordinate would have to do is to assert his or her inner power, or to withdraw.

Sometimes subtler innuendos are implied by the self-appointed oppressor. A superior tone of voice, a raised eyebrow, or other insidious embellishments can superciliously suggest that no reasonable person would disagree with what he or she has to say and that the only decent thing for the listener to do is to defer to the conventional wisdom of the other's assumed authority. If we accept this unspoken injunction, we are sure to feel helplessly dominated.

When our first priority is to take charge of ourselves, we are less likely to experience this avoidable sense of helplessness. If, instead, our primary goal is to control other people by inhibiting their disapproval, we are certain to find ourselves subject to their power ploys.

So here is yet another paradox of power, whether we are the ones who have power or those who don't, any attempt to take advantage of others puts us at risk. As W.C. Fields used to say, "You can't cheat an honest man." While this adage may be something of an exaggeration, it's true that at those times when we try to control other people, we are most susceptible to being exploited by them.

Usually we are spared entrapment in webs of power that make helpless submission our only alternative. However, there are times when it is necessary to resist other people's defining our relationships and presuming to have authority over us. For example, when we express an opinion in a public situation, someone may challenge our assertion in an officious manner, saying, "What right do you have to say something like that? It was impolite, uncalled for, and unkind. That's the sort of statement that can only make the rest of us feel bad."

If we insist that we had not meant to be inconsiderate, we are meeting the challenge on our adversary's turf and we are likely to end up looking bad for having spoken out at all. If, instead, we try to convince them that what we said was not rude, we come off looking stubborn and insensitive. In either case, whether or not they forgive us, we end up feeling helpless and are reduced to protesting apologetically that we meant no harm. We appear all the worse for having accepted the power of their assertion in the first place and then arguing against it.

When we retain the inner power of taking charge of ourselves, we have more viable alternatives. We are free to redefine the relationship by firmly pointing out that in challenging our opinions as not being nice, the other person is confusing manners with morals. Or we need not take his or her definition of our relationship seriously. Instead we can laugh off the attempt at domination by pointing out that a revolution is not a teaparty.

When we redefine the power structure of a relationship, it need not serve as a disadvantage to either party. This is clear in my work with psychotherapy patients. Many of the impasses that arise are needless power struggles between myself and the patient.[3] Most often they begin when, unwittingly, I try to pressure the patient into doing something that he or she is not yet ready to attempt. It is up to me to recognize my own contribution to this tangle, to give up trying to control the patient's life, and to settle for simply taking charge of the therapy.

Outside of therapy as well, many of our unhappy struggles with other people—even with those we love—are the outcome of our trying to control one another. Each of us attempts to turn the other into what we want him or her to be. The first step in resolving such struggles is attending to how our own needs to control have contributed to the impasse. Ironically, if there is to be a resolution, it is the "older child" who needs to give in. Whichever of us is most aware of his or her own part in creating the trouble between us must be the first one to take responsibility for giving up trying to change the other.

If, after carefully examining our own motives, we still believe that the sole source of the problem is the outcome of our partner's attempt to control us, then it is time to redefine the relationship. For example, when we disagree, the other person may mistakenly take my opinions as a put-down against which he or she must defend by accusing me of being harsh and judgmental. When my protests to the contrary go unheard, I am free to join the resistance by exaggerating the other person's accusations as follows, "You must be right. The only reason I ever talk to you at all is to try to make you look foolish. I must really hate you or I wouldn't humiliate you every chance I get." If my paradoxical intention is successful, my partner will end up laughing in protest that I'm not really *that* bad and perhaps sometimes all I intend is an honest effort to iron out a disagreement.

There are some power struggles that we cannot resolve without willingly going against our grain by admitting that, although we know better, we go on contributing to the trouble between us. For example, every marriage entails some of the same arguments repeated again and again over the years. Whatever the content of any particular squabble, basically these battles of wills hinge on differences in personality style. Ironically, when these same dissimilarities between partners are not dreadfully clashing to control one another, they compliment each other delightfully.

There are times when I am arguing with my wife and I know that what I am about to say next is exactly the same thing I always say that only makes matters worse. I vow that this time I won't make the same dumb mistake. Instead, for once, I'll just shut up. A moment later I am horrified to hear my mouth spewing forth exactly what I told it not to say.

At times like these when it is myself I cannot control, I sometimes resort to employing one paradox to resolve another.

This left-handed approach is a homeopathic, hair-of-the-dog healing in which like cures like. In certain instances, a thorn can be used to remove another thorn, a second poison can serve as an antidote to the first, and one paradox can resolve another. When you are unable to exercise the self-control you intend, try taking charge by allowing yourself to imagine willfully indulging your need for omnipotence. Think about what it would be like to tell the person with whom you're struggling, "What I really want is to have everything my own way all the time. I want to control you so completely that you willingly comply with all my desires without my even having to ask." If this paradoxical approach doesn't free you in a given situation, for the time being you may have to settle for being stuck. Wait and try again in the next power struggle you get into.

At those times when I cannot control myself (let alone anyone else), I find it useful to remember the following tale:

> When Prince Mou of Wei was living as a hermit in Chungsan, he said to the Taoist Chuang Tzu, "My body is here amidst the lakes and streams; but my heart is in the palace of Wei. What am I to do?"
>
> "Care more for what you have in yourself," said Chuang Tzu, "and less for what you can get from others."
>
> "I know I ought to," said the prince, "but I cannot get the better of my feelings."
>
> "If you cannot get the better of your feelings," replied Chuang Tzu, "then give play to them. Nothing is worse for the soul than strug-

gling not to give play to feelings it cannot control. This is called the Double Injury, and of those that sustain it, none live out their natural span."[4]

If you can't give up, give in!

12

You're Telling Me!

For all of August and the early part of September, I grant myself the rest and recreation of a long restorative annual vacation. Ironically, it is during this deliberate period of recuperation that I become fully conscious of just how physically handicapped I actually am.

Ordinarily, I intentionally escape this excruciating awareness. As one aspect of my careful and comprehensive attempts to remain in charge of both my personal and my professional life, I have modified my physical environment to meet my personal needs. My autumn/winter/spring world has been tailored to deflect unnecessary experiences of overwhelming powerlessness that are otherwise elicited by head-on encounters with my physical limitations. But the place where my family and I spend our summer vacations is an uncompromisingly primitive setting that resists modification of its rough terrain to compensate for my handicaps.

Each August I return to our island for the ritual restoration that accompanies resumption of my romance with the sea.[1] As I said in *Buddha*, again and again, the living waters draw me back to their shores to instruct me about all that is changelessly ever-changing. The ocean is both endlessly calm and disruptively turbulent, quieting my own inner turmoil while, at the same time, insistently warning me of the dark powers that lie unquiet beneath both the water's surface, and my own.

As I stand alone at the ocean's edge, I experience myself as its master. For a moment, it is my vision that defines the universe. All at once, my ephemeral omnipotence is overwhelmed by the vast expanse of sea and sky. As if through God's eye, I see myself as no more than a pitiful speck at the edge of a cosmic puddle.

If I remain open to its tidal rhythms, the sea inevitably puts me in touch both with the ebb and flow of my own special singularity, and with the ordinariness of my trivial existence. Great South Beach runs the length of the island—much of it almost empty of people. This lower edge of Martha's Vineyard is bounded by a stark backdrop of looming, red clay cliffs. As they approach the long, narrow shoreline, they are buffered by gently declining yellow dunes that gradually become more and more sparsely greened by beach grass. The yellowish white sands of the beach slope down to the edge of the ever-changing, never-changing green-blue-black of the shifting sea. Hanging overhead is a moving white-on-blue montage of clouds blowing across a vast open expanse of sky.

In the past, I spent long languorous sunny days, watching the unending build-up and release of ocean waves along the unpeopled edge of those many miles of pristine, seabreeze swept beaches. I walked the boulder-strewn shoreline in search of stones, shells, and other seaside treasures. At the pleasure of the tides, I swam the smooth and easy swellings of the sea, or rode its wildly cresting, loudly crashing breakers.

Like the sudden winter storms that wear away the island's edge, years of illness and neurosurgical ordeals have eroded my body, limiting both my physical power and my freedom of movement. Since the onset of my illness, each subsequent summer exposes that year's hidden increase in my helplessness.

Again and again, I promise myself that the following August I will be better prepared. Yet every summer, these isolated island beaches once again catch me off-guard.

My impaired sense of balance makes the uneven slope, unyielding stones, and unpredictable currents of ocean beach terrain agonizingly awkward to maneuver. The unblinking eye of my partially paralyzed face is painfully vulnerable to the once soothing sea-breezes. Diminished coordination of my left side leaves me incapable of swimming in the sea whose siren song I was once unable to resist. As if all these restrictions were not enough, a recent bout of skin cancer adds a caution against spending any extended time in the sun, no matter how sedentary.

Although I am powerless to overcome most of these restrictions, I remain unwilling to relinquish the pleasure of our Augusts on the island. My family and I continue to summer in that preciously primitive setting, and I make whatever accommodations I must.

I spend more time than before on the beach-house deck overlooking the waters of the Vineyard Sound. The island has always been a place, where for some time each day, I have read, written, and listened to music. I regret that these activities now occupy more of my vacation than they once did. Many days, I no longer venture out to my beloved, but unforgiving ocean. Instead, I carefully tread down to the Sound's tamer and more sheltered seascape where the breezes are more gentle, and the waves less wild.

Old friends from other parts of the country also vacation on the Vineyard. Early in our lives, they were year-round neighbors. Now we rarely see them, except in summer when we get together on the island. I take more quiet time with them than now than I did on earlier vacations.

Best of all, recent Augusts offer the fun of reunited close family living. We refer to our colorful clan as "just the eleven of us" (my wife and I, our three sons, two daughters-in-law, and four grandchildren). Because I am so easily exhausted on these vacations, I've disqualified myself completely from previously shared household chores.

I am learning to allow myself and others who care about me to cater to my being a partial invalid. Accepting my frailties allows me to indulge myself appropriately, to ask others for help, and to allow them the pleasure of doing for me some of the tasks that have become too difficult for me to do on my own.[2] And, God willing, in this island setting, gradually and gracefully, someday I'll be able to accept fully just how helplessly handicapped I can sometimes be.

This August marks my twentieth year of illness. Over the years, additional handicaps have left me more and more helpless. I once had seemingly endless energy available for playing with my sons. Now, though I still enjoy the playful antics that go on while living with the young families of these long-grown children, I tire all too easily.

As I write of all the accommodations I must make to the unrelentingly rough terrain of our island retreat, I realize that it is not the sudden stormy assaults of illness alone that have ravaged my physical power. The everyday erosion of ordinary aging is yet another inevitable tide that cannot be turned.

Growing older requires my being a *mensch* about its insidious inroads into my physical power as well. Although I can control neither sickness's sudden batterings of my body, nor aging's gradual erosion of my strength, I am determined to remain in charge of how I live my life. Whenever I am able to recognize that I have no other choice, I feel freer to accept my helplessness more easily.

Only God knows what He had in mind when He graced us all with gradually growing old and eventually dying. Why He should have chosen me in particular to endure decades of debilitating illness, I have no idea! Who needed all this special attention? It's fine with me when, once in a while, He chooses someone else. If, God help me, I have the audacity to be completely honest about how I feel, I have to admit that it's an honor that I could have done without!

Who among us can make sense of the wisdom of His ways? If, on the one hand, having had more than my share of handicaps is nothing more than the result of a statistical error on His part, then it doesn't mean a thing. But if, on the other hand, He has chosen me personally to a search for meaning in these accursed experiences, then the test of my faith is finding some message hidden in this awful mess!

What can I tell you? What can I tell myself? Sorting through sufferings to try to transform garbage into a compost heap is not my idea of keeping the covenant. It's certainly not a job for which I would have volunteered.

I have been assigned the task of making something worthwhile out of the awful experience of being incapacitated by illness. Even though I didn't make this mess, it's my responsibility to clean it up. While I'm at it, I may as well try to find whatever I come across that seems worth passing on to my children.

What am I to tell them? It would be foolish for me to admonish that they should stay well. It also wouldn't help if I advised them, "Never grow old!" What would be the point? Even when a parent only wants what's best for them, *children never listen.*

I can only hope that watching how I've lived my life has been of some use to them. It would be blessing enough if having had to see me suffer could at least offer them the counsel of the little I have learned about coping with powerlessness.

My wish is only that they might understand that *personal power doesn't come from trying to control external events and other people.* A person cannot do what cannot be done. Life is not a matter to be managed. We have little influence on its outcome. Our only impact lies in how we live it. We didn't ask for the responsibility of taking charge of ourselves, but its the only power to which we are entitled. And, in the end, no matter how well we have prepared, the moment belongs to God.

From my position as patriarch, I suppose I could try enlightening our sons, their wives, and even our innocent grandchildren. I could take them aside separately, and instruct each one:

"At times, your life will get out of control. There will be undeserved troubles, disappointments, illnesses and injuries. If it's not one thing, it's another! Some suffering cannot be helped. Complain all you like about how helpless you feel! That won't work either.

"No matter how hard you try to live right, sometimes God will grant you a mess so unmanageable that it will seem impossible to endure. It can't be helped. No matter how helpless you feel, it's no use arguing with Him. For that matter, there's no point in blaming anyone else. Even if it wasn't you who made the mess, you're the one who has to clean it up."

Knowing my family, I can only expect that each of them would patiently hear me out. And then, with a cynical raise of an eyebrow and an ironic shrug of the shoulders, each would answer:

"You're telling me! "

A List of Some Truths about the Paradoxes of Power That May or May Not Be Worth Knowing Because in the End . . .
The Moment Belongs to God

1. Rock breaks scissors, scissors cut paper, paper covers rock. Power depends on the situation.

2. Everyone has dreams of triumph and fantasies of humiliation.

3. No matter how powerful we are, or think we are, some people are stronger.

4. However powerless we may feel, others are weaker.

5. Sometimes life is so out of control that there is nothing we can do to make things right.

6. Self-esteem based on feeling powerful is weak. Inevitably life exposes us and the pain seems unbearable.

7. Be confident that you will continue to make mistakes.

8. Whether we have too much or too little, power is always a problem.

9. The excessive use of power may ruin what you set out to improve.

10. The freedom to do as you please is one kind of power.

11. Coping with helplessness is another.

12. We must give up trying to control others.

13. Inner power comes from loving others, not from being loved.

14. We must temper appreciation for power when we have it with respect for others when they don't.

15. We must learn to take responsibility for both our power and our helplessness. It sounds simple, but it isn't easy!

16. It takes one kind of courage to wait patiently and another to get on with it.

17. In our right pocket we need to keep one reminder: "For my sake, God created the universe," and another in our left pocket: "I am dust and ashes."

18. There is no way for any of us to be totally on top of every aspect of our lives.

19. We will only succeed some of the time. The only thing we can do is keep trying.

20. No one is ever totally safe from harm.

21. Willingness to risk can bring rewards we can't get otherwise.

22. If we choose to run scared, our capacity for love is limited.

23. Timid lives are terribly dull.

24. If we learn to tell false alarms from real ones, we can decide which risks are worth taking.

25. When we deal with fear, the way out is in.

26. Without trust, we can't accept the intimacy of gently holding another's trembling heart in our hands, or placing ours in theirs.

27. We're all helpless when it comes to predicting what will happen next.

28. None of us feels safe being completely open.

29. If no one knows you, who can love you?

30. Denial increases the dangers of what we fear.

31. Too often we form negative attachments rather than face the fear of being alone.

32. Inner power has less to do with pleasing others than it does with doing as we please.

33. Defying or complying with authority has nothing to do with living freely.

34. We don't have the power to make someone love us.

35. Laughter is the sound of freedom.

36. Sometimes there's nothing we can do but wait.

37. We will all be fools at times. When we accept that, our imagination opens to possibilities we were once too wise to consider.

38. If it's not one thing, it's another.

39. Life is not a matter to be managed.

40. A person can't do what can't be done.

41. Like Life, Death makes fools of us all.

42. None of us can afford to miss the opportunities for the freedom to take charge of ourselves and to laugh and enjoy what we can.

43. However well we may prepare, the moment belongs to God.

Notes

Prologue

1. Derived from Bertolt Brecht's "Some Stories about Herr Kauner," in *Brecht on Brecht*, trans. George Tabori (New York: Columbia Records, 1963).

Chapter 1

1. Wu Ch'eng-en, *Monkey*, trans. Arthur Waley from the Chinese, originally titled *Journey to the West* (New York: Grove Press, 1958).

Chapter 2

1. Lord Acton, *Essays on Freedom and Power* (Boston: Beacon Press, 1948), 365.

2. Adlai Stevenson, a quote from *The Observer*, 1963, reprinted in *A Dictionary of Modern Quotations*, ed. M.J. Cohen (Baltimore: Penguin Books, 1971), 219.

3. Philip G. Zimbardo, "The Psychological Power and Pathology of Imprisonment," *Selected Documents in Psychology, Ms. No. 347* (Washington, D.C.: American Psychological Association Journal Supplement Abstract Service, 1973).

Chapter 3

1. Erving Goffman, *Asylums: Essays on the Social Institutions of Mental Patients and Other Inmates* (Garden City, New York: Doubleday, 1961).

2. For the sake of simplicity, I will refer to the child as male and to the mother as female, although obviously both the infant and the primary parent may be of either gender.

3. David McClelland, *Power: The Inner Experience* (New York: Irvington Publishers, Inc., 1975).

4. Lao Tzu, *The Way of Life*, trans. Witter Bynner (New York: Capricorn Books, 1944), 63.

Chapter 4

1. Idries Shah, *The Pleasantries of the Incredible Mulla Nasrudin* (New York: E.P. Dutton, 1971).

2. Sheldon Kopp, *Who Am I . . . Really?: An Autobiographical Exploration on Becoming Who You Are* (Los Angeles: Jeremy P. Tarcher, Inc. 1987). Pages 147-182 contain a detailed account of my twenty-year struggle with a brain tumor.

Chapter 5

1. Colin Turnbull, *The Mountain People* (New York: Simon & Schuster, 1972).

2. Anna Freud and Dorothy T. Burlingham, *Infants Without Families*, Medical War Books (New York: International Universities Press, 1944).

3. Elie Wiesel, *The Gates of the Forest*, trans. Francis Frenaye from the French (New York: Holt, Rinehart and Winston, 1966), from the introduction.

Chapter 6

1. Mendele Mocher Seforim, *The Travels and Adventures of Benjamin the Third*, trans. Moshe Spiegel from the Yiddish (New York: Schocken Books, 1968).

2. Sheldon Kopp, *Raise Your Right Hand Against Fear: Extend the Other in Compassion* (Minneapolis: CompCare Publishers, 1988).

Chapter 7

1. I am indebted to James Hillman for his explorations of the Jungian archetypes of youth and aging (the *puer* and the *senex*). See the anthology he edited, *Puer Papers* (Irving, Texas: Spring Publications, 1979).

2. *est* is an acronym for the Erhard Seminars Training, perhaps the most commercially successful of the quick-fix, mass-group therapy residuals of the Human Potential Movement's encounter experiences. Typically, an *est* training session involves 250 people at a time, in consecutive weekend marathons billed as "sixty hours that transform your life."

3. Idries Shah, *The Sufis*, with an introduction by Robert Graves (New York: Doubleday, 1971), 225.

Chapter 8

1. I.L. Peretz, "Bontsha the Silent," in *Selected Stories*, trans. Hilde Abel, ed. Irving Howe and Eliezer Greenberg (New York: Schocken Books, Inc., 1974), 70-77.

2. Ibid., 20-24.

3. Ecclesiastes ("The Preacher"), chapter 12 of the Old Testament.

4. This all took place before I myself had become physically handicapped.

Chapter 9

1. Isaac Bashevis Singer, "Gimpel the Fool," in *The Collected Short Stories of Isaac Bashevis Singer*, trans. Saul Bellow (New York: Farrar Strauss Giroux, 1983), 3-14.

2. Desiderius Erasmus, *In Praise of Folly*, ed. and trans. Hoyt Hopewell Hudson (New York: Random House, 1941).

3. Ibid., 35.

4. Walter Kaiser, *Praisers of Folly, Erasmus, Rabelais, Shakespeare* (Cambridge, Massachusetts: Harvard University Press, 1963), 8.

5. Conrad Heyers, *Zen and the Comic Spirit* (Philadelphia: Westminster Press, 1973), 44.

Chapter 10

1. Sholem Aleichem, *Favorite Tales of Sholem Aleichem*, trans. Julius and Francis Butwin (New York: Avenel Books, 1983). Tevye later became the central character of the successful American stage play and film *Fiddler on the Roof* by Joseph Stein.

2. Mark Zborowski and Elizabeth Herzog, *Life Is with People: The Culture of the Shtetl*, with an introduction by Margaret Mead (New York: Schocken Books, 1952).

3. Ibid., 149.

4. Rabbi Hillel, quoted in *Chapters of the Fathers*, with a commentary by Rabbi Pinhas Kehati, trans. Rabbi Abraham J. Erlich and Avner Tomaschoff from the Hebrew (Jerusalem: Department for Torah Education and Culture in the Diasporah of the World Zionist Organization, 1984), 41.

5. Elie Wiesel, *One Generation After*, trans. Lily Edelman and Elie Wiesel (New York: Avon Books, 1972), 94ff.

Chapter 11

1. Fyodor Dostoyevsky, *The Brothers Karamazov*, trans. Andrew H. MacAndrew with an introductory essay by Konstantin Muchulsky (New York: Bantam Books, 1981), 297-319.

2. Luke 4:1-13.

3. Sheldon Kopp, *Back to One: A Practical Guide for Psychotherapists* (Palo Alto, California: Science and Behavior Books, 1977), Chapter 7, "Impasses," 103-114.

4. Arthur Waley, *Three Ways of Thought in Ancient China* (New York: Doubleday, 1956), 48.

Chapter 12

1. Sheldon Kopp, *If You Meet the Buddha on the Road, Kill Him!* (Palo Alto, California: Science and Behavior Books, 1972), 152-159.

2. See Adolf Guggenbuhl-Craig, "The Archetype of the Invalid," in *Eros on Crutches: Reflections on Amorality and Psychopathy*, trans. Gary V. Hartman from the German (Irving, Texas: Spring Publications, 1980), 12ff.